BIBLE STORY POEMS
Genesis - Ruth
By: Darrell Scott
Joy Concepts
2021

For other books by Darrell Scott
Go to:
amazon.com/author/darrellscott

ALL ILLUSTRATIONS ARE PUBLIC DOMAIN

INTRODUCTION

Darrell Scott lost his daughter, Rachel Joy Scott, in 1999 when she was the first student killed in the Columbine High School shootings.

Darrell has spoken to over 5 million people in live settings not counting the millions that have seen him on Oprah, Fox News, CNN, Dateline, Good Morning America, and on the cover of Time Magazine.

He traveled for Campus Crusade and spoke in over 100 college and university campuses to record crowds from Texas A&M to Princeton.

He and his wife, Sandy, founded "Rachel's Challenge", a nonprofit organization that has reached over 28 million students, parents, and educators in live presentations. They have received 3 television Emmy Awards from Rachel's story.

The poems in this book were all written by Darrell. Some are humorous, and some are thought provoking. They all provide a great supplement to your sermons, or talks.

Each poem is followed by scripture verses that are connected to it. All of these Bible stories are from the books of Genesis through Ruth. All illustrations are in the public domain.

GENESIS TABLE OF CONTENTS

Bible Chapters	Title	Page
	THE BIBLE	10
Genesis 1-3	When God Split an Adam	13
Genesis 1	Divine Ways in Seven Days	16
Genesis 4	Raisin' Cain	18
Genesis 4	Cain's Pain	19
Genesis 5	Old Folks	20
Genesis 6	Huge Dudes	21
Genesis 6-9	Boat Man	22
Genesis 9	The Drunk and the Punk	24
Genesis 10	Stranger Danger	25
Genesis 11	Babblin' in Babel	26
Genesis 11	Power Tower	26
Genesis 12-13,19	Salty Lady	27
Genesis 12	Abe's Babe	28
Genesis 21	Haggard Hagar	30
Genesis 22	The Ram Exam	31
Genesis 24	The Tale of a Well and a Pail	32
Genesis 27	Expensive Soup	34
Genesis 28-29	Stairway to Heaven	36
Genesis 29	The Belle at the Well	38
Genesis 32-33	Wrestlemania	40
Genesis 37-47	Joe and the Dream Team	42

EXODUS TABLE OF CONTENTS

Exodus 1-2	Basket Baby	49
Exodus 3-5	Bushes, Snakes, and - - Mistakes	51
Exodus 5-9	The Pest with a Request	54
Exodus 11-14	Passover	58
Exodus 14-15	Water Logged	61
Exodus 15-17	Bitter Water – Bitter People	63
Exodus 17	God Smites the Amalekites	67
Exodus 18	A Pa-In-Law's Law	68
Exodus 19-32	You're So Special	69
Exodus 32-34	Moses Vents and God Repents	71

LEVITICUS TABLE OF CONTENTS

Leviticus 1-27	Leviticus	74
Leviticus 10	Naughty Boys	75
Leviticus 24:10-13	Don't Get Stoned	76

NUMBERS TABLE OF CONTENTS

Numbers 1-5	Numbers	78
Numbers 6	The Plight of the Nazarite	79
Numbers 11	Nose Vomit	80
Numbers 12	Miriam's Folly	81
Numbers 14	Wise Spies and Gutless Guys	82
Numbers 16	Korah's Challenge	84
Numbers 17	Nutty Staff	85
Numbers 20:1-13	Mission Unaccomplished	86
Numbers 20:14-21	Family Feud	87
Numbers 20:22-29	Deceased High Priest	88
Numbers 21:4-9	Israelite Snake Bite	89
Numbers 22-24	Just Listen to Your Ass	90
Numbers 25	Bellyache Mistake	92
Numbers 27:18	Nun Fun	93
Numbers 27:12-22	Transition	94

DEUTERONOMY TABLE OF CONTENTS

Deuteronomy 1-34	Deuteronomy	96

JOSHUA TABLE OF CONTENTS

Joshua 1-2	The Harlot and the Scarlet Cord	98
Joshua 3	Crossover	100
Joshua 4	Rocks in the River	101
Joshua 5:2-9	Ouch!	102
Joshua 6	No Mo' Jericho	103

JOSHUA TABLE OF CONTENTS (continued)

Joshua 7	Achan's Folly	105
Joshua 8:1-28	Ambushed	107
Joshua 9	The Plight of the "Ites"	108
Joshua 10	Paralyzed Skies	109
Joshua 11-12	Thirty-one to Nothing	111
Joshua 14-24	Two Legends	112

JUDGES TABLE OF CONTENTS

Judges 1	Thumbs and Toes	114
Judges 2	Judges	115
Judges 3	The First Three Judges	116
Judges 4-5	Jay and Debbie	118
Judges 6-7	Small is Better	119
Judges 8	The Wimp is a Warrior	122
Judges 9	Abimelek the Wreck	123
Judges 10	Grandpa Dodo	125
Judges 11	Awful Oath	126
Judges 12	Deadly Lisp	128
Judges 13	Disappearing Stranger	130
Judges 14	The Riddle	131
Judges 15:1-6	Flaming Foxes	133
Judges 15:8-20	Weaponized Jawbone	134
Judges 16:1-8	Sleazy Dates and Heavy Gates	135
Judges 16:4-21	Fatal Attraction	136
Judges 16:4-21	The Fox and the Locks	138
Judges 16:4-21	Weak and Bleak	138
Judges 16:4-21	Bad Date	138
Judges 16:21-31	Goodbye Samson	139
Judges 17-18	The Man Who Robbed His Mom	141
Judges 19-20	Obtuse Abuse	143
Judges 21	Stolen Brides	144

RUTH TABLE OF CONTENTS

Ruth 1	Orpah and Oprah	146
Ruth 2	Boaz is Smitten	148
Ruth 3	Flirtin' for Certain	149
Ruth 4	Schemer and Redeemer	151
About the Author		153

THE BIBLE

Some people think the Bible is an old, archaic book
If you are one – then, just for fun, please take another look
There's stories you will laugh at and there's some that bring you tears
There's drama, humor and romance, and there's hope and doubt and fears

There's criminals and animals - there's lions, snakes and bears
There's epic tales of great romance[1], and sordid brief affairs[2]
There's talking donkeys[3], talking snakes[4]- there's lice n' frogs n' locusts[5]
Intriguing tales of giant men[6], and there's some hocus pocus[7]

A lion kills a prophet[8] and a mighty tower falls[9]
Great fires consume a city[10]- warriors piss against a wall[11]
A serpent raised upon a stick[12] heals people who are bitten
A man and maid meet at a well[13] and both with love are smitten

The walking dead are in the streets[14], and iron axes float[15]
A fish will swallow up a man[16], and Noah builds a boat
Two bears will maul some naughty boys[17](It really was their fault)
Some ravens feed a hungry man[18]- A lady turns to salt[19]

A naked man would walk around[20], there's more that can't be stated
Some things would make a sailor blush, but they are all X-rated[21]
A lady boils and eats her son[22]- a man escapes from jail[23]
And water comes out of a rock[24]- and then there's Jezebel

There's gates that came from oyster's pearls[25]- A sea made out of glass[26]
A long haired dude kills many with the jawbone of an ass[27]
I could go on forever but I think that you'll concede
The Bible isn't boring - it's a fascinating read

So from this rhyme, please take the time, and give another look
At all the stories you will find inside this grand old book

10

ALL THE VERSES BELOW ARE FROM THE KJV

1. Song of Solomon
2. II Samuel 11
3. Numbers 22:28
4. Genesis 3:4
5. Exodus 8-10
6. Genesis 6:4
7. Exodus 7:8
8. I Kings 13:24
9. Genesis 11
10. Genesis 19:24
11. I Kings 16:11
12. Numbers 21:8
13. Genesis 29:10
14. Matthew 27:52
15. II Kings 6:6
16. Jonah 1:17
17. II Kings 2:24
18. I Kings 17:6
19. Genesis 19:26
20. Isaiah 20:3
21. I Samuel 18:27
22. II Kings 6:29
23. Acts 12:9
24. Exodus 17:6
25. Revelation 21:21
26. Revelation 15:2
27. Judges 15:15

11

GENESIS BIBLE POEMS
12

WHEN GOD SPLIT AN ADAM

"In the beginning" it says, "God created"
Now there is a statement that's often debated
Some say it was accident, luck, or just chance
While many believe it's a creative dance

The first thing God said was to "Let there be light"
He created day and he created night
He gathered the waters and called them "the seas"
He then made the shrubs, and the plants and the trees

With lights in the heavens for signs and for seasons
For warmth and for light and for various reasons
He put fish in the water and birds in the air
And beasts in the field like the lion and bear

But something was missing, and God couldn't rest
Until he'd created the thing he loved best
He knelt in the dirt and he played with the dust
Until in his image he created US!

Adam was sculpted by God's mighty hand
A master production - the very first man
But Adam was lonely and wanted a date
So, God performed surgery and made him a mate

Now God was the first to split open an Adam
And that operation produced the first madam
She'd been in there ribbing him all of his life
And now Eve emerged as his beautiful wife

God placed them in Eden - a true Paradise
They'd stay there unless they ignored His advice
He gave them one rule that they must never break
If they disobeyed, it would be a mistake

He'd planted one tree that they couldn't eat from
They'd die if they did - that would really be dumb
But then guess what happened - the first chance they had
They ate of its fruit - they were both very bad

13

The devil appeared as a serpent to Eve
And twisted God's Word while he tried to deceive
The serpent said, "You shall not die - God was kiddin'"
So, Eve ate the fruit that was plainly forbidden

She gave some to Adam and he ate it too
And then something happened - they suddenly knew
That they were both naked and needed some clothes
And that was the moment the Lord God had chose

To ask them "Where are you?" And Adam replied
"Lord, we are both naked and needed to hide"
Now God wasn't fooled 'cause He knew all along
That Adam and Eve would decide to do wrong

Our God has a purpose - a glorious plan
And even our failures are all in His Hand
So, Adam blamed Eve and then Eve blamed the snake
And they both admitted they'd made a mistake

Then God told the snake that on dust he'd be fed
And Adam's descendent would bust up his head
Now this is a promise that really should please us
At Calvary 'ole Satan was busted by Jesus

He then turned to Adam and Eve who were grieving
And told them the sad news that they would be leaving
Someday we'll eat fruit from the good Tree of Life
But first we'll encounter some pain, death, and strife

So, they left the Garden of Eden that day
The angels were ordered to send them away
But that's not the end of this short little story
It's just the first step to God's grace and His glory

So don't be too angry and don't pout or grieve
For that big mistake made by Adam and Eve
It didn't shock God 'cause He knew that they would
He knows how to turn all the bad into good

14

Now Romans 8:20 and verse 21
Reveals who was really behind what was done
Adam and Eve and the snake just fulfill
A piece of the puzzle in God's perfect will

'Cause out of the grave their great-grandkid would rise
And conquering death he would open the skies
To show us the things that we don't understand
Revealing God's glory and His perfect plan!

BIBLE VERSES:
Genesis 1:26-3:21   II Cor. 11:3
Rom. 8:20-21   I Tim. 2:13-14

DIVINE WAYS IN SEVEN DAYS

The seven days of God's creation hide a deeper plan
A spiritual unfolding for the life of every man
At first God said, "Let there be light" - and darkness had to flee
That light now shines within our hearts, allowing us to see

But light will just uncover all the things that darkness hid
And everything was still a mess, so here is what God did
He separated water from the land and called them 'seas'
That separation must precede the flowers, grass, and trees

The theme revealed the second day was all about division
For us to grow the Bible says there must be an incision
For Hebrews 4 verse 12 declares, the Sword of God will sever
Separating soul and spirit, freeing us forever

And so, the Word of God divides our spirit from our soul
Our life will then be fruitful, and our spirit be made whole
The third day of creation brings us fruitfulness and seeds
Allowing us to reproduce the spirit's words and deeds

The third day in Galatians 5 shows what that fruit can do
Producing love, and peace and joy, and faith, and meekness too
Without the light and separation fruit could never grow
Each day is purposely designed - a planned, progressive flow

The fourth day God created all the stars, the moon and sun
But God knew it was not complete - He'd only just begun
The sun, and moon, and stars were there for light and other reasons
He put them there to govern and to guide - for signs and seasons

As soul and spirit separated fruitfulness occurred
His Spirit started guiding us, we're governed by his Word
Maturity is taking place in our unfolding story
And we are growing in his grace, from glory unto glory

16

The fifth day brought us liberty and freedom all can share
The fish and birds are gliding through the water and the air
And every creature flowing in the sea and in the air
Depicts the freedom that our God allows us all to share

The sixth day he created all the lions, bears and such
But there was something else to make - it was his crowning touch
He placed his finger in the dust and then created man
For Adam was designed to be the center of his plan

And this applies to you and I - each step was so designed
From light to separation - then to fruitfulness we find
That guidance, governance and freedom weren't the final goal
Conforming to his image would fulfill our destined role

The purpose of day six was to be changed into his image
God put us in the game of life - this isn't just a scrimmage
But there is one day left before the cycle is complete
The final step is taken when we're resting at his feet

Each day that he created is advancement for our good
Each step along the journey has a purpose, as it should
But on the seventh day we find that all God did was rest
And although every day was great - this day would be the best!

BIBLE VERSES: **Genesis 1**

17

RAISIN' CAIN

Now Adam and Eve had a son they named Cain
Who worked in the field with the corn and the grain
They then had another boy - they named him Abel
He worked with the sheep and kept meat on the table

Now God had rejected an offering from Cain
But Abel's was blessed, and it drove Cain insane
His anger was raging and soon he would kill
His young brother Abel while out in the field

Now Cain was in trouble and soon it got deeper
He said to the Lord "Am I my brother's keeper?"
Then God spoke to Cain and said, "I'll bring you down
Your poor brother's blood has cried out from the ground"

"I'll send you away from your family and home
And all through the earth you will wander and roam"
Then Cain said to God, "You are surely aware
My punishment, Lord, is just too hard to bear"

Cain reaped what he sowed when he disobeyed God
He soon had to leave for a place that's called 'Nod'
Poor Adam and Eve - they were nearly insane
Cause now they'd lost Abel and couldn't raise Cain

BIBLE VERSES: **Genesis 4:1-15   Hebrews 11:4**

18

CAIN'S PAIN

Soon after Cain killed Abel, he would wander all around
He lived with guilt and sorrow; Abel's blood cried from the ground
He said to God, "My punishment is more than I can bare"
He knew he was unworthy to approach the Lord in prayer

But God, who shows us mercy would give Cain another chance
He put a mark upon him with a warning in advance
Should any try to kill him, then Jehovah would step in
His vengeance would be seven-fold, they'd take it on the chin

So, Cain in desperation left the presence of his God
And moved far east of Eden to a place that he called "Nod"
Before too long he found a wife, and children soon would come
It makes you wonder, where in thunder was this lady from?

And who went to their wedding? These are things that puzzle me
Was she his younger sister - did she blossom from a tree?
Oh well, we may not ever know, but one thing is for sure
We never even knew her name, so she remained obscure

So, Cain would build a city and would name it for his son
Now Enoch was his firstborn, but was not his only one
But Enoch's kids would innovate with creative intentions
Producing things like bronze and iron and musical inventions

But Cain's one deed of wickedness forever ruined his name
He'd join the list of people all remembered for their shame
There's Judas, Hitler, Al Capone, there's Genghis Khan and Stalin
And right there at the very top - Cain joins those who have fallen

BIBLE VERSES: **Genesis 4:8-19**

19

OLD FOLKS

When folks have lived for ninety years, they're old, without a doubt
But back in Bible times those folks would just be starting out
Take Adam, at a hundred thirty he would have a son
To us that's old, but not to him, he'd only just begun

Eight hundred years he'd go on living after Seth was born
At nine hundred and thirty years he died, so aged and worn
Yes, quite a few lived nine full centuries - that's what you call old
These guys were young at just five hundred if the truth be told

Methuselah would live the longest, but he too would die
At age nine hundred sixty-nine he'd seen a lot go by
His grandson would be called of God, and chosen by his grace
Yes, Noah would construct an ark and save the human race

But he would live 500 years before he even started
And labored hard a hundred years before the ark departed
If you feel old and feeble, and you think your life is done
Remember folks from Bible times, 'cause you have just begun!

BIBLE VERSES: **Genesis 5:3–32, Genesis 7:6**

HUGE DUDES

Now Adam's great granddaughters would elope with sons of God
Their kids would all be giants - (Which to me seems rather odd)
Sometime before the ark was built these mammoths roamed around
Their awesome feats were legendary - men of great renown

Some versions of the Bible call these monsters, "Nephilim"
There's many untold stories that we'll never hear from them
These giant men of mighty deeds no longer can be found
'Cause Noah's flood would wipe them out and all of them were drowned

BIBLE VERSES: **Genesis 6:4**

21

BOAT MAN

The people were wicked, but God had a plan
He chose to use Noah - a good, righteous man
"Now Noah, I want you to build a big boat
It's gotta be done right or else it won't float"

"So go build three decks with one window and door
And make sure you fill all the cracks in the floor"
So, Noah began with his blood, sweat, and tears
A project that took over one hundred years

But people made fun of what Noah was doing
He heard them all laughing, and jeering, and booing
His 3 sons helped build it and so did their wives
That hundred-year stretch took a chunk from their lives

Then finally they finished that gigantic ark
And God said to Noah, "Now go to the park"
"And gather the animals - choosing the best
Seven of some and two each of the rest"

There were zebras and monkeys and lizards and hogs
Antelope, cheetahs, hyenas, and dogs
Rabbits and tigers and lions and rats
Crocodiles, possums, gorillas, and cats

Oh, what a parade as they marched up the ramp
And into the ark which would be their new camp
And then came the rain as the Lord let 'er rip
The ark was now floating - they'd started their trip

For forty long days and for forty long nights
Ole Noah's big fear was about the termites
He kept them in cages and fed them tree bark
'Cause if they got loose, they could eat up the ark

22

The water kept falling like ten million fountains
Until it had covered the tops of the mountains
Now, inside the ark they were doing quite well
(Unless you considered the horrible smell)

And finally the rain stopped and Noah's ark sat
On top of the mountains of old Ararat
The smell got so bad that on Noah's agenda
The first thing he did was to open a window

He sent out a dove who flew back with a leaf
And when Noah saw it he smiled with relief
That meant that the waters had finally gone down
And soon they'd be leaving the ark for dry ground

The humans were ready - the animals too
For over a year they had lived in that zoo
And finally, God opened the door with His Hand
And they all poured out to inhabit the land

They worshipped Jehovah and offered him praise
And all of the animals went separate ways
Then God said to Noah, "I promise, my friend
The whole world will never be flooded again"

And then as a sign that the whole world may know
He put in the clouds a bright, shiny rainbow
So, each time you see one you really should showa
Magnificent smile and remember ole Noah!

BIBLE VERSES: **Genesis 6-9 Matthew 24:37 Luke 17:26
II Peter 2:5 Hebrews 11:7**

THE DRUNK AND THE PUNK

The flood had come and gone at last - the waters had receded
God promised through a rainbow - it would never be repeated
So, Noah and his family left the ark to start anew
They were the only ones alive, and they were just a few

Ham, and Shem, and Japheth were his sons who would embark
To fill the earth with people now that they were off the ark
But Noah had a vineyard that he tended to with care
He loved to plant and harvest grapes out in the open air

But then one day he drank some wine and got intoxicated
He lay there naked in his tent - a man inebriated
Then Ham walked in and with a grin, he made fun of his dad
He told his brothers he had seen him drunken and unclad

But Shem and Japheth were ashamed and reprimanded Ham
The way he'd treated their old dad was nothing but a sham
They took a garment, and they went to where their father lay
They backed in there to cover him - their heads were turned away

When Noah gained his consciousness and heard what Ham had done
He felt both anger and dismay toward his foolish son
A blessing came from Noah, he bestowed on Ham's two brothers
But Ham and his descendants would be cursed to serve the others

BIBLE VERSES: **Genesis 9:15 - 27**

STRANGER DANGER

There once was a hunter, a great, mighty man
The Bible just mentions him twice
Of Nimrod we're left with an incomplete scan
To hear more - just might have been nice

First Chronicles one and in Genesis ten
He's given a brief little push
It doesn't say much about Nimrod, but then
We know that his dad's name was Cush

BIBLE VERSES: **Genesis 10:8-9   I Chronicles 1:10**

25

BABBLIN' IN BABEL

The builder of Babel did say,
"You men build an entrance this way
A solid oak door, up on the 8th floor"
But God changed their language that day

"Please hand me a hammer – be quick"
He turned and was handed a brick
He asked for a nail – was handed a pail
"My helper", he thought, "must be sick"

"Young man, you were hired for the chore
Of helping me put up this door
Now hand me a plank – and quit looking blank"
The reply – "Ees no savvy, Senior!"

BIBLE VERSES for both poems: **Genesis 11:1-8**

POWER TOWER

The people said, "Let's build a tower
We'll start on it this very hour!"
But when almost complete
God wiggled His feet
And shook the thing down with His Power!

26

SALTY LADY

When Abram and his nephew, Lot, decided to disband
Young Lot would go to Sodom - Abraham to Canaan land
Their servants couldn't get along, and there was no debate
Although they still were family they would have to separate

Now Sodom was an evil town, a very wicked place
So, God decided to remove his mercy and his grace
Two angels came to visit Lot and warned him to avoid
The fire that God was sending for the town would be destroyed

An angry mob surrounded Lot - they wanted to attack
His visitors but they had no clue how angels can fight back
Their motives were so evil - their intentions were unkind
They made their move, but when they did, the angels struck them blind

They then told Lot to get his wife and daughters and leave town
'Cause everything in Sodom would be burning to the ground
The angels told them, "You must run, or you will not survive
If you look back, or if you're slack, you just won't be alive

But Lot's wife chose to disobey, and coming to a halt
She quickly took a backward look, and she would turn to salt
So, if you're tempted to do wrong, or even something shady
Remember Lot and his poor wife, who's now a salty lady

BIBLE VERSES: **Genesis 12:4, 13:5-14, 19:1-23**

ABE'S BABE

Now Abe had a visit from God one spring day
For he had been chosen to go far away
The Lord said, "I'll bless you and make your name great
And any who curse you will not like their fate"

"Through you all the nations of earth will be blessed"
But first Abe would go through a difficult test
Now he was no young-un, in fact he was old
At seventy-five he was hardy and bold

To start on a journey because of God's Word
His friends at the nursing home thought it absurd
Their first stop was Egypt - a land hot and dry
Where Abraham told his wife Sarah, to lie

They told the Egyptians that she was Abe's sister
The king started flirting and soon he had kissed her
Then God struck old Pharaoh with plagues that same day
And Abe learned a lesson - to lie doesn't pay

Now Pharaoh got angry and started to shout
He told his commanders to boot them all out
So, Sarah and Abram and his nephew, Lot
Went right out of Egypt and bought them a plot

Now Abe's and Lot's servants were not a good fit
So, Abe said to Lot, "I just think we should split"
It seems their relationship really hit bottom
So, Lot chose to go to the city of Sodom

Then God said to Abram, "Now listen to me
And lift up your eyes – 'cause as far as you see
I'll give you the land everywhere that you roam
Your many descendants will call it their home

28

Now Abram was old, and these words made him sad
Cause he had no children - no one called him "Dad"
So Sarah told Abram to father a son
With Hagar, her servant - and so it was done

And they named him 'Ishmael' - but he could not stay
Cause Sarah was jealous and sent him away
When Abe was a hundred his wife would conceive
And give him a son - it was hard to believe!

So, Isaac was born and now Abraham knew
That there wasn't anything God couldn't do
Through Isaac's descendants the world would be blessed
Long after Abraham laid down to rest

BIBLE VERSES
Genesis 12-21:20 Hebrews 11:8-12 Galatians 3:14

HAGGARD HAGAR

Hagar was haggard and weary and worn
Her heart was so heavy, her will had been torn
She'd only obeyed what her masters had said
And now they forsook her and wanted her dead

They forced her to leave with her son by her side
And out in the desert they both may have died
'Cause Abram and Sarah now had their own son
And young Ishmael's purpose was over and done

God promised to Abram that he'd have a boy
And Sarah used Hagar – a devious ploy
'Cause Sarah was old, and she couldn't believe
That God could enable her womb to conceive

And even when angels confirmed that she would
She laughed at the thought that she actually could
But then came the miracle – Isaac was born
And from that day on Hagar felt Sarah's scorn

And so, they had left, and they could not return
Their welfare was no longer Abram's concern
Her son was abandoned – and it was absurd
All simply because – Sarah doubted God's word

BIBLE VERSES: **Genesis 21:1-14**

THE RAM EXAM

Jehovah God decided he'd give Abraham a test
He asked for him to sacrifice the thing that he loved best
God said, "You must do what I say - don't hesitate or falter
Take Isaac up the mountain and then place him on an altar

Collect some wood and take a knife and offer up your son
Go sacrifice him in the fire before three days are done"
So, Abraham took Isaac and two servants up the trail
He felt like this whole thing was just a morbid fairy tale

Then Isaac said, "We have the wood, but we don't have a lamb"
"God will provide for us my son", replied old Abraham
He built an altar, took his son who he had tightly bound
He took the knife and raised it up and almost brought it down

But then an angel startled him - he yelled for him to stop
The angel pointed to a bush and said, "It's time to swap"
Release him now and go look in that thicket up ahead
And you will find a ram that you can sacrifice instead

So, Abraham and Isaac took that ram and sacrificed
It was a future pattern for the death of Jesus Christ
'Cause God said, "You were willing to give up your only son
And someday I will do the same before my plan is done"

"Your kids will number like the stars, or sands upon the shore
And I'll protect and bless them all, for now and evermore"

BIBLE VERSES
Genesis 22:1-18

31

The TALE of a WELL and a PAIL

Now Abraham decided that his son should have a wife
He really was aware that he was near the end of life
He gave instructions that were clear, not leaving it to fate
He sent his servant far away to find the perfect mate

The lady must be willing to go back to Canaan land
For Isaac could not move away, because of God's command
His promise was to bless them in the place where they now dwelt
And Isaac could not violate what he had heard and felt

The servant traveled many days and as the evening fell
Young ladies came with jars of clay to fill them at a well
The servant asked the Lord for help, he said, "If I should ask
For water, let the right girl say, 'I'll gladly fill the task"

"And also, for my camels, let her ask for them as well
To quench the thirst of all of us with water from her pail"
And just when he had finished asking God for this request
A beautiful young lady, who stood out from all the rest

Approached him with a friendly smile and said, "How do you do?
I'll gladly get some water for your camels and for you"
He stood there in amazement with his stomach feeling queasy
He hardly could believe that it had happened just that easy

She said, "My name's Rebekah and I live quite close to here"
He told her he had traveled far, and then he made it clear
"I've come to find a pretty bride for Isaac, who's my master
I really hope my journey will not end as a disaster"

The servant took a golden ring and placed it in her nose
(The practice isn't quite as new as some of us suppose)
He gave her golden bracelets that she wore around her arm
The servant knew that Isaac would be captured by her charm

Jacob went back home with her where he would meet her mother
He also met a man named Laban who was Becca's brother
He then explained why he had come - they listened soberly
Rebekah's mom just nodded and replied, "Sounds right to me"

However, they requested that she stay for ten more days
The servant sighed, then, he replied, "There must be no delays"
They all turned to Rebekah who would answer soft and slow
"I know that this is from the Lord, so yes, I choose to go"

They traveled back to Canaan and a wedding soon took place
'Cause Isaac knew the moment that he saw Rebekah's face
That he was totally in love - and so our story ends
Just trust in God and do his will - it pays big dividends

BIBLE VERSES: **Genesis 24:1-66**

EXPENSIVE SOUP

Rebekah talked to Isaac and they both agreed that maybe
They should start a family - it was time to have a baby
And so, a little boy was born, but soon he would reveal
That there was yet another one just clinging to his heel

Now Esau was the older son, a red and hairy guy
He loved to hunt, and fish and camp beneath a starry sky
Rebekah favored Jacob more, there wasn't any doubt
He hung around the house all day and seldom ventured out

One chilly day, when skies were gray - young Jacob made some stew
And Esau smelled it from outside and said, "I want some too"
Now Esau, as the oldest owned the birthright from his dad
And that's the one thing Jacob always wanted really bad

So, Jacob turned to Esau, and he made a proposition
He said, "I'll spare a bowl of soup, but there is one condition"
"And what is that?" Esau replied, "What's in this deal for you?"
"If you give me your birthright, you can then have all the stew"

"Well, I'm so hungry I could die - let's do this" Esau said
"It makes no sense for me to own a birthright if I'm dead"
So, Esau swore to Jacob, and the trade-off was complete
Then Jacob got his birthright, while his brother ate some meat

But Jacob wanted more than just the birthright he'd received
For him to gain the family blessing, dad must be deceived
Now Isaac's eyes were getting bad, and he could hardly see
So, Jacob and Rebekah hatched a plan of treachery

Then Isaac said to Esau, "I would like to have some meat
Go take your bow and arrows - bring me something back to eat"
"And then the family blessing, I'll bestow by my own hand
And all of your inheritance - the flocks, the tents, the land

34

And that is when Rebekah chose to go on the attack
She said to Isaac, "Get two goats and quickly bring them back
And while your brother's hunting, I'll make Isaac's favorite stew
Instead of blessing Esau, he will end up blessing you"

Now Jacob's skin was very smooth - his countenance was pale
If Isaac tried to touch him, this whole scheme was doomed to fail
'Cause Esau was a hairy man with little grace or charm
So, Becca took a goat skin and she covered Jacob's arm

The time had come to fool his dad, and steal the blessing too
And, sure enough, his dad would ask, "Now Esau is that you?
"Your voice sure sounds like Jacob's, but I feel your hairy skin
My ears must be deceiving me, so I will just begin"

And raising up his voice to God, old Isaac blessed his son
"Prosperity will follow you, your wishes will be done
And nations will bow down to you, and kings will kiss your feet
And those who bless you will be blessed - your life will be complete"

But as he finished talking, take a guess at who walked in?
Yep – Esau now was ready for his blessing to begin
And when he heard what happened, he became an angry man
Because his younger brother had deceived him once again

But Jacob, in his later years would reap what he had sown
For he would be deceived by his own sons when they were grown
So just remember that your lies may end up hurting you
And let your actions be for good, and let your words stay true

BIBLE VERSES: **Genesis 27:1-36**

STAIRWAY TO HEAVEN

Now Jacob, son of Isaac, took a trip and traveled far
(Back then the trip was longer, 'cause he didn't have a car)
By sundown he was getting tired, and so he made a bed
He had no fluffy pillow, so he used a stone, instead

He went to sleep and had a vision - here is what he dreamed
A stairway was ascending into heaven, so it seemed
And angels traveled up and down this stairway to the sky
They seemed a bit too far away for him to ask them why

When suddenly a man appeared above the angel crowd
"I am the Lord your God" he said - his voice was really loud
"I'll bless you and your children - they will spread across the land
To west and east and north and south, and everywhere they stand"

"And all the people of the earth are blessed because of you
The world will know that you are mine, for what I say is true"
The dream drew to a close and Jacob slowly came awake
He lay there in amazement - it was quite a bit to take

He said "The Lord was in this place - his presence was so near
I saw his holy angels, and his words were loud and clear"
Then Jacob took his pillow stone, anointing it with oil
And then he called it Bethel, saying, "This is holy soil!"

"If God will help me get back home, providing what I need
Then I will serve him all my life - he is my God, indeed"
And as he helps me prosper - ten percent of what I own
I'll gladly give back to the Lord from gratitude alone

He started on his journey, and it led him to a well
But that's another story that I don't have time to tell
The point I'd like for you to know about this stairway deal
Is that our God is always there despite what we may feel

The feeling of his Presence may not always be around
But he will never leave you, and his promises are sound
The stairway isn't always seen - But it is there indeed
The Way, the Truth, the Life is here, supplying all we need

BIBLE VERSES
Genesis 28:10 – 29:3

THE BELLE AT THE WELL

Now after Jacob had his dream he came upon a well
But it was covered by a stone - quite heavy, he could tell
A group of shepherds brought their sheep right over to the brink
The stone still set atop the well, so none of them could drink

He asked them if they knew his Uncle Laban, who lived near
They said to Jacob, "Yes, in fact, his daughter's coming here"
When Rachel finally got there, she walked right up to his side
And Jacob knew without a doubt that she would be his bride

He felt a rush of energy and rolled that stone away
He then leaned in and kissed her - on the lips! Oh, happy day!
Some goose bumps popped up on his arm - There must have been a dozen
And then to her complete surprise, he told her, "I'm your cousin"

She ran back home and told her dad, and Laban made a fuss
"You are my flesh and blood", he said, "So you will stay with us"
So, Jacob started working for his uncle on the farm
He stayed there for a month and then, he mustered up his charm

"I love your daughter, Rachel with my heart and with my soul"
Now Laban, who was crafty knew that he was in control
He said to Jacob, "Work for me for seven years and then
The marriage will take place for you - my daughter's hand you'll win

The seven years flew by so fast, because he was in love
He thought of Rachel as a gift from heaven up above
But when the wedding happened, he was in for a surprise
He ended up with Leah, who had problems with her eyes

Now Jacob was a bit upset - his happiness had burst
But Laban said, "The rule is clear - the oldest marries first"
But if you want to marry Rachel here's what you can do
Just work another seven years and you can have her too

So, Jacob buckled down and worked another seven years
These went a little slower, and he shed a lot of tears
But finally, he fulfilled his dream, and Rachel was his wife
She filled his heart with purpose, and she brightened up his life

Sometimes we just can't understand the way that God provides
He always knows what best for us - and He - - not us, decides
And why He does things His own way, sometimes we cannot tell
So don't reject his blessing when a belle comes to your well

BIBLE VERSES: **Genesis 29**

WRESTLEMANIA

Jacob had deceived his dad and stolen from his brother
And so, he fled and traveled to the hometown of his mother
He now was married, with two wives, and prospered very well
And everything was going right as far as he could tell

Now Jacob wanted to return to Canaan, but he knew
His brother, Esau, and his clan all lived in Canaan too
And Esau had declared that he would kill him if he could
Because of what he'd done to him, he knew his brother would

Despite his fears, he made the choice to head to Canaan land
His herds, and servants, wives, and kids - they made up quite a clan
They carried gifts to offer Esau, hoping he'd be kind
Then Jacob sent them all ahead, but he would stay behind

An angel then appeared to him and challenged him to fight
They wrestled and they fought, and this went on throughout the night
Then Jacob grabbed the angel and he held him in his grip
The angel then reached down and touched the socket of his hip

The angel crippled Jacob's leg, but couldn't break away
He said, "I have to leave before the dawning of the day"
But Jacob firmly shook his head and said, "The answer's 'No'
I need for you to bless me, or I'll never let you go"

The angel sighed and then replied, "So tell me, what's your name?
I'll bless you but I'll change it and you'll never be the same"
So, Jacob became Israel which means something very odd
The meaning of his name is, "One who wrestles with his God"

The next day, he'd meet Esau and the two would make amends
From that day on they would be known as brothers and as friends
But all of their descendants would see things a different way
The fighting and hostility remain until this day

Marciano, Sugar Ray, Mohammed Ali too
Norris, Tyson, Jones, and Frasier, just to name a few
Great fights have been recorded, but when all is said and done
Jacob and the angel's fight would rank as number one

BIBLE VERSES
Genesis 32-33

41

JOE AND THE DREAM TEAM

Young Joe was a boy who was loved by his dad
Since Joe was the favorite - his brothers were mad
'Cause Jacob, their father, had made Joe a coat
Of bright rainbow colors and it got their goat

Then Joe had a dream where their sheaves all bowed down
To his sheaf of wheat with their heads to the ground
The dream made them angry, but Joe wasn't through
The sun, moon, and stars would all bow to him too

Joe stupidly told them - a major disaster
They thought he was saying that he was their master
Then Jacob warned Joe, "Just be careful my lad
Your visions are making your brothers all mad

His brothers were angry and started to scheme
Of how they could terminate Joe and his dream
So, one day they grabbed him and lowered him down
Inside a small cave that was under the ground

He sat in that cave while they finished a meal
Then traders came by, and they all made a deal
His brothers then pulled him up out of the cave
And traded poor Joseph - he now was a slave

They took him to Egypt where he would be sold
And Potiphar bought him for pieces of gold
Now meanwhile his brothers would take Joseph's coat
And rip it and dip it in blood from a goat

"Wild animals killed him", they told their old dad
They showed him Joe's coat and poor Jacob was sad
Now Potiphar, Captain of Pharaoh's command
Soon saw that our Joe was an honest young man

He'd leave and ask Joe to take charge as his double
But Potiphar's wife soon got Joe in deep trouble
She flirted with Joseph with Potiphar gone
But Joe pushed her off, 'cause he knew that was wrong

Rejected and angry she started to yell
And Joseph soon found himself locked up in jail
Were you ever right - but were misunderstood?
Sometimes we can suffer for doing what's good

If that ever happens to you - don't give in
When you have done right, you'll eventually win
So even in jail Joe became a succeeder
That jailer put Joseph in charge as a leader

'Cause right there in prison our God had a scheme
To introduce Joe to the local Dream Team
It turns out, the baker, and some other guy
Had made the king mad (And please don't ask me why)

They shook and they shivered and knew they were dead
When Pharaoh was yelling, "Go cut off their head"
But soon he calmed down and just threw them in jail
But guess where they landed? In Joseph's own cell

Now they had a dream on that very same night
They both were dejected and shaking with fright
Now God had shown Joseph the truth in their dream
Sometimes things just aren't quite as bad as they seem

But then on the other hand sometimes they're worse
The baker would soon find that out in this verse
The cupbearer's dream showed him serving the king
And Joseph assured him that, "That very thing

Will happen – in three days they'll let you go free!
So please don't forget to tell Pharaoh of me"
The baker was happy, "They'll let me go too!"
But Joseph looked sad as he said, "I'm not through

Your dream was of baskets of bread on your head
But three days from now you will hang 'till you're dead!"
Ends and beginnings to God are all known
And everything happened the way Joe was shown

The ungrateful baker was really a snot
The promise he made to poor Joe – he forgot
Then one summer night he remembered his vows
When Pharaoh had dreams of a field full of cows

The king called magicians and all his wise men
But none of them knew what to do – but just then
The cupbearer hollered, "Oh listen great king
A Hebrew named Joseph can help with this thing"

He then cleared his throat, and he went on to tell
Of he and the baker and Joseph in jail
"Go get him this moment!", ole Pharaoh did scream
They brought Joseph back to interpret his dream

"The next seven years we'll have harvests of plenty
Then followed by seven when we won't have any"
"The Lord says to store up the corn and the grain
He'll give an abundance of sunshine and rain"

The king was impressed with what Joe had to say
He made him a leader in Egypt that day
Now Joseph got married - his family would thrive
Manasseh and Ephraim soon would arrive

The first seven years were just great - like Joe said
The eighth year brought famine and soon it had spread
Beyond all of Egypt it kept right on gainin'
Until it had covered the farmlands of Canaan

Now all of Joe's brothers and Jacob, his dad
We're starving in Canaan, the famine was bad
So, Jacob said, "Boys you can stay here and die
Or else go to Egypt - there's food you can buy"

So, he sent his sons down to Egypt for grain
Just hoping their journey would not be in vain
Their journey was destined - as strange as it seems
To bring a fulfillment to Joe's early dreams

The dream that his brothers would bow down before him
He now ruled in Egypt - they couldn't ignore him
And so, it would happen, when they came to town
To Joseph, their brother they all would bow down

But they didn't recognize Joe when they came
Of course, he was grown and did not look the same
He asked where they came from and to their surprise
He said to his brothers, "I think you are spies"

46

They told him they all came from Canaan for food
But Joe asked more questions - he seemed very rude
They told him their dad and their young brother stayed
But Joseph seemed angry, and they were afraid

He told them again that He thought they were spies
And he was unhappy with all of their lies
They all were confused and could not understand
That Joseph had secretly made up a plan

There's more to this story, but I don't have time
To give every detail and make it all rhyme
'Cause after a while, Joseph cried like a child
His family came back - they were all reconciled

In Genesis forty-five, please read verse eight
'Cause that is the lesson I'd like to relate
It wasn't Joe's brothers who did all this to him
But God – who had purposed to work all this through him

The Lord wants us all to forgive one another
To love and be kind to our sister and brother
God's ways are mysterious - past finding out
But faith in his Word will remove every doubt

Have faith and be thankful in all that you do
And next time you're angry, or moody, or blue
Remember ole Joe who was Egypt's redeemer
And don't be afraid if God makes you a dreamer!

BIBLE VERSES
Genesis 37, 39-47   Hebrews 11:22

47

EXODUS BIBLE POEMS

48

BASKET BABY

Soon after Joseph passed away a new Pharaoh appeared
The Israelites became his slaves, the thing that they all feared
He then would give an order that was horrible and vile
Each baby boy, once he was born, was tossed into the Nile

The Hebrew girls would all be spared, they didn't pose a threat
But boys could turn to warriors, something Pharaoh might regret
And so his fear compelled him to commit atrocious deeds
But God would bring his judgment through a baby in the weeds

A Levite woman had a son and fearing for his life
She hatched a plan to save him, so she grabbed a carving knife
She cut and formed a basket that would float along the Nile
She coated it with tar and pitch and tested it awhile

"Oh God protect my little boy", she fervently would pray
She pushed the basket through the reeds and watched it float away
She waited for the miracle - she hoped God would deliver
And then it happened – Pharaoh's daughter walked down to the river

And right before her very eyes an infant floated by
The Pharaoh's daughter was amazed and gave a startled cry
She told here servant, "Grab that basket - bring that little boy"
And when she held that infant child her heart was filled with joy

49

She knew he was an Israelite, but now he was her son
She gave her slave a message and she sent her on the run
"Go find a Hebrew lady who is motherly and calm"
And guess who she would bring back? It would be the baby's mom!

"We'll disregard my dad's commands - this order he imposes
We'll save this little Hebrew boy, and we will call him 'Moses'
Because we took him from the water - that will be his name
He'll be a part of royalty and share our wealth and fame"

But Pharaoh's kingdom would collapse and soon he would be dead
For God would use his grandson to bring judgment on his head
The enemy would like to steal, and kill and to destroy
But always be reminded of this little baby boy

BIBLE VERSES
Exodus 1:8 – 2:9

BUSHES, SNAKES, and PHARAOH'S MISTAKES

Now Moses lived in Egypt where his family all were slaves
But Pharaoh's daughter tutored him on how a prince behaves
She saved him as a baby, and she raised him in the palace
But he observed that Pharaoh treated Israelites with malice

One day as he was watching Hebrew slaves perform their work
He saw an angry supervisor acting like a jerk
He hit a Hebrew slave and then he watched him slowly die
And Moses grew so angry that he gave a savage cry

He jumped on that Egyptian guard and beat him to the ground
He killed the man with his own hand then quickly looked around
He hoped no one was watching but he didn't see a soul
He grabbed a shovel, dug a grave, and threw him in the hole

But someone did see Moses, and the Pharaoh was upset
He ordered guards to take his life, but Moses heard the threat
He ran away to Midian and sat down by a well
He'd managed to escape the guards, as far as he could tell

Then seven lovely ladies just appeared around the block
They came up to the well so they could water all their flock
Some local bullies told the ladies that they couldn't stay
But Moses used his kung foo and he chased them all away

The ladies took him home with them and he would marry one
Then he and his wife, Zippy soon would have their firstborn son
Now Moses needed work and so he started herding sheep
He worked all day and worked all night and hardly got much sleep

But meanwhile back in Egypt, wicked Pharaoh soon would die
The Israelites had prayed for help and God had heard their cry
And so, he chose old Moses who was tending to his flock
The way that God appeared to him caused Moses quite a shock

An angel in a burning bush that never was consumed
Began to speak to Moses who I'm sure thought he was doomed
The Lord said, "Moses, Moses" - who replied, "Lord here am I"
Then God revealed that he had heard the Hebrews fervent cry

"Take off your shoes" God said to him, "For this is holy ground
And I am calling you today to something quite profound
I'm sending you to Egypt where you'll set my people free
You'll lead them all to Canaan land where they will dwell with me"

"And when they ask who sent me", Moses asked, "Who shall I say?"
The Lord replied, "Just say, 'I AM' and they will be okay"
But Moses wasn't quite convinced and so he pressed ahead
"But if they don't believe me - they may laugh at me instead"

"Okay", said God, "Then take that staff you're holding in your hand
And throw it on the ground and soon you'll come to understand"
So, Moses threw his staff down and it turned into a snake
It scared poor Moses half to death - his knees began to shake

52

"Now pick it up", God said to him, "Just grab it by the tail"
"You're kidding", Moses then replied - his face was turning pale
He closed his eyes and grabbed it - he was nearly scared to death
It hissed then turned back to a staff while Moses held his breath

Then God said, "Moses, here's another trick that I've devised
Just stick your hand inside your coat and you will be surprised
So, Moses did as he was told, but needed therapy
'Cause when he did what God had said his hand had leprosy

Then God reversed the process, and his hand was fully healed
But Moses didn't like this stuff and wasn't very thrilled
He told the Lord, "I'm not the guy - send anyone but me
When I see snakes, I get the shakes, and I hate leprosy

Now God was somewhat ticked at Moses, but he finally said
"Okay, but get your brother, Aaron, I'll use him instead"
And so, to Egypt they would go with all their kids and wives
Their family didn't want to go, all fearing for their lives

They met the Hebrew elders when they got to Egypt land
Where Aaron did the magic tricks, and followed God's command
The elders were so grateful that Jehovah heard their prayer
They all bowed down and worshipped with their hands up in the air

However, the new Pharaoh wasn't ready for God's word
He laughed at Moses and at Aaron, calling them 'absurd'
"I'll never let the Hebrews free, no, not a single one"
But God would make him willing by the time this tale is done

Next time you see an angel in a bush that's set aflame
You might just want to listen if he's calling out your name
Don't close your eyes, or shut your ears, or choose to be offended
The end result will always be the thing that God intended

BIBLE VERSES: **Exodus 3:1-5:6**
53

THE PEST WITH A REQUEST

Now Moses went to Pharaoh with a merciful request
But Pharaoh looked at Moses as an irritating pest
"You think that I will let my slaves just simply walk away?
You must be nuts – go tell your God that this is where they'll stay"

"Not only will I keep them here, but now because of you
I'll make them work much harder and I'll give them more to do"
He told his overseers, "Keep the quota for their bricks
But make them gather their own straw, those lazy Hebrew hicks"

The Hebrew slaves were angry, and their elders said to Moses
"You irritated Pharaoh - we can't do what he proposes
Our workload doubled over night because of your endeavor
So, thanks a lot, your stupid plot has made things worse than ever"

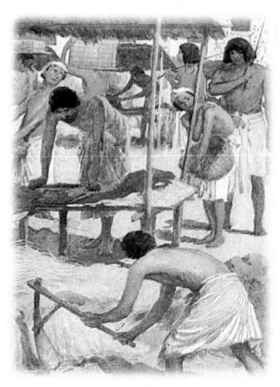

54

Then Moses spoke to God again, "I told them what you said
But Pharaoh and the elders both would love to have my head"
The Lord said, "Moses, chill my man and watch what I can do
I'll set the Hebrew children free, and they will follow you"

And Pharaoh will be glad to say, "You slaves are free to go"
But Moses wasn't quite so sure - and told Jehovah so
"I'll take my brother, Aaron, and we'll try it once again
But he's a stubborn king - and Lord, my faith is getting thin"

They both went back to Pharaoh who could not believe his eyes
He said, "I told you 'no' before - what is it with you guys"
Then Aaron threw his staff down and it turned into a snake
And Pharaoh laughed and said to him, "That trick is just a fake"

He called for his magicians, and he told them what to do
And so, they threw their staffs down and they turned to serpents too
But Aaron's snake just turned and ate the ones that they had thrown
The wise men and magicians knew their secrets now were blown

But Pharaoh's heart was hardened, and he wouldn't change his mind
So, Aaron did another trick, but Pharaoh still declined
The water of the Nile was turned to blood and really stunk
The odor from the dying fish was worse than from a skunk

The next day Aaron raised that staff and frogs were everywhere
In soup and shoes and clothes and booze and everybody's hair
And Pharaoh said, "I've had enough, I'll let the Hebrews go"
But once the frogs had all expired, he changed his mind to "No"

Then Aaron took that magic staff and tapped it in the dirt
And from the dust a swarm of gnats produced a world of hurt
The king's magicians tried that trick but couldn't make it work
And Aaron winked at Moses with a twinkle and a smirk

However, Pharaoh still refused and firmly held his ground
Until the staff came out again and flies were swarming round
Once more he said that they could go, then once again he changed
And Aaron said to Moses, "Bro, that dude is quite deranged"

The king of Egypt wouldn't bend despite his losing battle
Their cows and sheep and camels died - their donkeys and their cattle
Then boils and hailstorms all appeared and caused much apprehension
And finally, locusts swarmed the land and got Pharaoh's attention

He first said "Yes", but then said "No" as he had done before
Then darkness came for 3 whole days, as black as miner's ore
Then Pharaoh called for Moses - he was raging when he said
"Don't ever come around again, 'cause if you do – you're dead"

Nine plagues and still no freedom – 'cause some folks just never learn
The final plague would end it, but would take a tragic turn
The firstborn children all would die - such sorrow it would bring
And all because of stubbornness from one Egyptian king

BIBLE VERSES: **Exodus 5:1 – 9:33**

PASSOVER

Now God had hardened Pharaoh's heart and he would not obey
He'd made it plain to Moses that the Hebrew slaves would stay
Nine awful plagues had come and gone, and Pharaoh would not yield
Because his heart was hardened, Pharaoh's firstborn would be killed

The tenth plague was an awful one, and soon it would arrive
The firstborn from each family and each flock would not survive
God said to Moses "Tell my people, they must be aware
. That death will visit Egypt so each family must prepare"

"And let them know it's time to go - I'm gonna set them free
So, everyone must pack their bags and be prepared to flee"
That night each family slew a lamb and roasted it to eat
But they were told to take the blood before they could retreat

And place it on the doorpost for Jehovah God declared
That when his angel sees the blood, your firstborn will be spared
That angel will pass over if the blood is there in sight
But back in Egypt every firstborn son will die tonight

In Egypt there was mourning, and the wailing would not cease
But back in Goshen no one died, their children slept in peace
As all of Egypt agonized, the tenth plague now was done
And Pharaoh grieved the loudest for he lost his firstborn son

The Israelites had served as slaves four hundred thirty years
Generations labored with their blood, their sweat, their tears
And now they tottered on the brink of total liberation
God had promised them a land where they could form a nation

And finally in his stricken grief the king told them to go
With such a massive group of people, traveling was slow
They packed their socks and led their flocks and headed out of town
They couldn't wait to close the gate - nobody hung around

Now Joseph many years before had made the Hebrews swear
That if they ever left the land, they'd take him out of there
And Moses had remembered so he did not hesitate
To carry Joseph's bones along inside a special crate

The Lord said, "I will lead them through the desert to the sea
And they will marvel at the way that I will set them free"
He promised that he'd guide them with a cloud throughout the day
And through the night a flame of fire would lead them on the way

But my dear friend, it's not the end of this fantastic tale
The Hebrews were about to see a miracle unveil
But first their biggest test would come, they'd get the third degree
Behind them was the devil and in front the deep blue sea

Sometimes our path will take us to a place of no relief
There seems to be no answer and our heart is full of grief
But out of weakness, strength appears, to set the captive free
And that's when grace and mercy can fulfill their destiny

BIBLE VERSES: **Exodus 11 - 14**

WATER LOGGED

When Pharaoh finished grieving for the death of his own son
He started having second thoughts about what he had done
He'd finally said to Moses that the Hebrews could go free
But one last time he changed his mind and gave a brisk decree

To gather all the chariots and warriors in the land
He'd give them all what they deserved - he'd crush this Hebrew clan
His slaves had all been gone a week, but couldn't be that far
They numbered in the millions and not one possessed a car

So, Pharaoh's army started out to bring the Hebrews back
They left a million footprints, so they weren't that hard to track
The Israelites were sitting ducks - this really would be fun
Between the army and the sea, there was no place to run

But meanwhile all the Hebrews were complaining to the Lord
"You led us here and now we'll die", they wailed with one accord
But Moses would rebuke them and continue to believe
That God was not quite finished, he had something up his sleeve

What lack of trust these people had - they'd seen God in the cloud
He'd led them with a flame of fire - they were a faithless crowd
But Moses knew that God was true, and stretching forth his hand
The Red Sea started parting and they traveled on dry land

61

Great walls of water stood up high - a path right through the sea
He ordered them to move ahead - not one would disagree
That must have been an awesome sight - a miracle for sure
And Moses felt a special thrill to lead them on this tour

I wonder if the fish would swim right through that liquid wall
And flop around upon the trail in front of one and all
Or if some child who acted wild would run his hand along
And pierce the sheet of water just to see if it was strong

Did someone cast with fishing rod - a lure right through the side
And snag a big ole trophy bass and hold it up with pride?
But Pharaoh still pursued them just as Moses knew he would
His army followed close behind to catch them if he could

Then God allowed their wheels to jam so it would slow them down
And most of Pharaoh's army were about to turn around
When Moses, (played by Charlton Heston) raised his hand again
Those massive walls of water buried all of Pharaoh's men

Some said the Red Sea got its name because of all the mud
But it would get much redder with Egyptian soldier's blood
The Israelites had been set free 'cause Pharaoh's men were dead
Their bondage finally over, and their shackles now were shed

So, someone started singing and the multitude joined in
A song of great deliverance for a new day would begin
The tambourines were banging, and their voices sang with glee
"Our Lord has cast the horse and rider down into the sea"

They all forgot their unbelief before the intervention
And how they murmured and complained with anger and contention
This pattern would emerge again - in fact for forty years
Each time the Lord would rescue them they'd celebrate with cheers

But when adversity arose their murmuring would start
The wilderness would soon reveal the hardness of their heart
In everything let's give God thanks - not just when problems cease
By faith we walk through valleys with a heart of total peace

'Cause he's the master *in* the storm - not just the master *of* it
His Word will guard our hearts and minds, if we can learn to love it

BIBLE VERSES: **Exodus 14 – 15:21**

BITTER WATER – BITTER PEOPLE

All Israel rejoiced when they crossed the Red Sea
'Cause Pharaoh had drowned, and they all were now free
They sang and they danced, and they all praised Jehovah
Their masters were dead, and their slavery was ova

But just three days later they grumbled again
Their water was gone, and their patience was thin
The desert was hot, and their throats were all parched
The sun was relentless wherever they marched

Then someone yelled, "Water!" and everyone ran
They rushed to the brink, and they knelt in the sand
The water was shining, the surface aglitter
But then they discovered the water was bitter

They all turned to Moses and started complaining
Their faces were angry their voices disdaining
And God was perturbed with their childish behavior
They failed to acknowledge that he was their savior

So, God said to Moses, "Their attitudes stink
Throw wood in the water and then they can drink"
They drank and were full and once more they gave praise
But still they were ignorant of God and his ways

They soon would leave Marah, to Elim they'd go
Where twelve springs of water continually flow
And seventy palm trees would offer them shade
And so, for a few days that's where they all stayed

But soon they would leave and start marching again
This time they would head through the Desert of Sin
But soon they were hungry and started to wail
And God in his mercy sent manna and quail

Now manna was bread that would gently float down
From out of the sky and would cover the ground
They ate all they wanted until they were fed
No hoarding allowed - it was just daily bread

The manna was free - there was no need for money
The taste was delightful like wafers and honey
But if they kept more than they needed today
Then maggots would cause all the food to decay

And Moses told Aaron, "Put some in a jar
This manna will someday become a memoir
Year later that jar would be privately hid
In the ark of the covenant under the lid

They camped at a place that they called Rephidim
They grumbled at Moses and argued with him
Once more they were thirsty, their circuits were fried
They just never trusted the Lord to provide

Jehovah told Moses, "Go stand by that stone
And don't be afraid 'cause you're never alone
I'm with you, so listen and do what I say
And all I expect is for you to obey"

"Now go strike that rock with the staff in your hand
And water will pour out to cover the land"
So, Moses obeyed and the rock split apart
Then water gushed out and the people took heart

Their thirst was now quenched, and you know the routine
They sang and rejoiced, and they put on a scene
They had problems with water the next forty years
But the cycle remained with their grumbling and fears

The lesson for us is to praise and give thanks
While going through problems when everything tanks
Quit griping and fussing and trust God instead
Be led by the spirit - not thoughts in your head

BIBLE VERSES **Exodus 15 – 17:5**

66

GOD SMITES THE AMALEKITES

While Israel was in Rhephidim, the Amalekites attacked
It came as a complete surprise, they all were shocked, in fact
And Moses said to Joshua, "Go conquer this riffraff
Tomorrow, help me climb that hill and I'll hold up my staff

That staff was quite impressive if you look back and recall
The frogs and boils, and lice and flies and Pharaoh's waterfall
The bitter water turned to sweet - the rock that broke away
That staff, with all its awesome deeds had quite a resume

And now it would be weaponized against the Amalekites
As long as Moses held it up it helped the Israelites
But when he lowered down the staff, they started losing ground
And when he raised it up again his army would rebound

His arms grew weary, from his age and weakened constitution
'Till Aaron and his buddy, Hur, came up with a solution
They found a stone and sat him down - to help the poor old guy
And then they stood on either side and held his hands up high

They stayed that way 'til sunset and the battle would be won
The Amalekites were beaten, and they finally turned to run
And after all was said and done, once more that staff came through
And Joshua was honored as a leader, tried and true

The lesson here is pretty clear - we can't triumph alone
Sometimes we just need help when we are weary to the bone
I once felt self-sufficient, but I've come to realize
The body gets its strength from that which every joint supplies

BIBLE VERSES: **Exodus 17:8-16**

A PA-IN-LAW'S LAW

Now Moses had a pa-in-law and Jethro was his name
He was a priest in Midian, a man of wealth and fame
He heard of all that God had done by his almighty hand
And so, he packed up all his stuff and went to join the clan

He watched as people came to Moses every single day
With all their problems and their pain to hear what he would say
He saw that Moses was worn out from all this endless chatter
So, Jethro sat and counselled him about this tiresome matter

He said, "Appoint some leaders who are able-minded men
Let some rule over thousands and let some rule over ten
Let some rule over hundreds and your workload will decrease
Let proper government arise and people will find peace

This noble man designed a plan that helped out everyone
And then he chose to go back home - he knew his work was done
So, Moses did as Jethro said - exactly to the letter
He implemented his advice and things were so much better

BIBLE VERSES: **Exodus 18**

YOU'RE SO SPECIAL

Just three months after leaving Egypt, Israel made a camp
The cloud was leading through the day, God's fire had been their lamp
They now were at Mount Sinai where much history would be made
And Moses climbed the rugged mountain, where he knelt and prayed

Now God began to speak to Moses - here is what he said
"Remind those grumpy Israelites about the quail and bread
Of how I broke their bondage and of how I set them free
I bore them out on eagles' wings and brought them back to me"

"Now if they will obey my voice and listen when I call
Then they will be a special people - treasured above all
They will be a priestly kingdom and a holy nation
All of Israel will be mine - a chosen congregation"

Now after Israel listened to what Moses had to say
They told him they would follow God and always would obey
God gave them all commandments - and he started out with ten
He knew that they would break his orders time, and time again

Don't covet, steal, don't curse or kill, and six more rules were there
And then a ton of minor ones would make them pull their hair
There's yearly feasts and Sabbath laws and punishments galore
Like drinking from a firehose, they just couldn't handle more

Then God called Moses up the mountain just to seal the deal
He wrote the 10 commandments on a stone to make it real
He stayed there forty days and nights and God showed him a plan
A pattern of the things that would reveal the Son of Man

A tabernacle was designed - its' furniture as well
Each piece created carefully with purposeful detail
A brazen altar would come first - a sacrificial place
Then followed by a laver holding water like a vase

Then seven golden candlesticks with seven lamps aflame
A table for the showbread that the Levite priests would claim
Then followed by a golden altar where incense would rise
And then there was a mercy seat where blood would symbolize

The coming death of Jesus who would sacrifice his life
Whose blood would take away all sin, removing guilt and strife
The final piece would be the Ark, it shone with golden gloss
The pieces all arranged into the image of the cross

God then gave him instructions - there were pages of this stuff
I'm sure that after forty days ole Moz had heard enough
The tapestries and hanging veils and badger skins and such
What priests should wear, and I declare, there really was too much

With Moses up the mountain, there was mayhem back in camp
'Cause Aaron, Moses' brother, was behaving like a scamp
He gathered all their earrings, and he made a calf from gold
These idiots were worshipping an idol from a mold

It's easy to look back at them and label them as flakes
But sometimes we forget that we repeat the same mistakes
We may not worship golden calves, but we can also fail
Unless we put our trust in God and let his love prevail

BIBLE VERSES: **Exodus 19 – 32:6**

70

MOSES VENTS and GOD REPENTS

While Moses was gone all the people complained
They wanted to play and to be entertained
They badgered poor Aaron, who quickly would fold
He gave them an idol - a calf made from gold

So, God said to Moses, "You'd better go down
'Cause Aaron, your brother is being a clown
I think I'll destroy them - consume them with fire
They're wretched and evil and need to expire"

But Moses confronted the Lord on that day
He pleaded for mercy - Here's what he would say
"You promised us freedom - don't change your intent
"I'm calling you out God, you need to repent"

"Egyptians will laugh when they hear what you did
They'll say you behaved like a little spoiled kid"
Your promise to Abraham - you cannot sever
You said that you'd bless his descendants forever"

And believe it or not, God repented that day
His anger died down and it all went away
So, Moses descended - but now *he* was mad
When he saw the idol - his temper got bad

He shattered the law that he held in his hands
The one God had written with all his commands
It's funny to me that despite his advancements
Poor Moses was first to break all ten commandments

He then took their calf and he burned it with fire
Rebuking them all for their wicked desire
He ground it all up and he sprinkled the powder
Out over the water and made them some chowder

71

He forced them to drink down the idol they'd made
I'm sure it was awful - not like lemonade
Then Moses asked Aaron, "Hey bro, what's with you?
I can't understand what you caused them to do"

And Aaron replied, with a bit of a pout
"I burned all their gold and this calf just jumped out!"
Then Moses called out, "Who will follow the Lord"
The Levites stood up - they were all in accord

And Moses commanded them, "Go out and slay
The Israelite men you encounter today"
And so they went out with their swords in their hand
And slew all the men based on Moses' command

Three thousand would die, spilling blood on the ground
The people of Israel were all feeling down
And God may have thought, "I should not have repented
'Cause Moses killed more than I ever intended!"

So back up the mountain ole Moses returned
He still was not happy that God had been spurned
Before he went up, he would make them all tackle
The chore of erecting a big tabernacle

Then God said to Moses, "I'll give you my grace
I'll show you myself, but you can't see my face"
He had Moses stand in the cleft of a rock
And gave him a peek as he circled the block

Then God said to Moses, "Take tablets of stone
And rewrite my laws which you broke on your own"
When we break God's law - when we falter and sin
He shows us his mercy, again and again

BIBLE VERSES: **Exodus 32 - 34:27**
72

LEVITICUS BIBLE POEMS

73

LEVITICUS

"Leviticus" sounds very strange to folks like you and I
Where is it from – what does it mean? You may be asking why
The third book of the Bible, it appears to be quite boring
If you should read it late at night, you may just end up snoring

The word means "Law of Levite priests" - those guys with robes and sandals
The ones who burned the incense and were always lighting candles
The list of offerings they would make was totally insane
The burnt, the sin, the fellowship, the guilt, and then the grain

And then there was the high priest - more important than the rest
He got to wear the Urim and the Thummim on his chest
Now you are probably asking, "What in thunder does that mean?"
Well, I can tell you, my dear friend, it's something really keen

The Urim and the Thummim were a part of the ephod
They helped the priest to understand when listening to God
Made up of many gemstones, they would light up in a way
That helped the priest interpret what Jehovah had to say

The animals they slaughtered, and the sacrifices made
The priests were set aside for God, they fasted, and they prayed
The laws, and feasts, and offerings are all spelled out for us
That's stuff you'll know, when ere you go to read Leviticus

BIBLE VERSES
Leviticus 1 – 27

74

NAUGHTY BOYS

Now Aaron was the high priest, but he had some naughty boys
They viewed the holy things of God as though they were their toys
They burned strange fire before the Lord which he had not commanded
They honored not his holy things and took them all for granted

So, God would send his holy fire and they would be consumed
Their lack of reverence for God would cause them to be doomed
Then Moses said to Aaron, "Bro, your sons have displeased God"
And Aaron didn't say a thing, he simply gave a nod

Then Moses would continue, "You must cover up your head
And rip your clothes, or I suppose you might just end up dead"
So, Aaron followed orders and gave offerings for their sin
God graciously forgave him and anointed him again

Although he would continue as the high priest all alone
He never would forget that both his boys were dead and gone
Because they had been foolish it would break his heart in two
For, after all, they were his sons - Nadab and Abihu

BIBLE VERSES: Leviticus 10

DON'T GET STONED

A woman named Shemolith had a trouble-making son
Her husband was Egyptian whom the Israelites would shun
Their boy got in a fight one day and used God's name in vain
In Israel, that was blasphemy and something quite profane

The law required that he be stoned and so, he had to die
Outside the camp, they took this lad - his family standing by
And all the crowd would be required to stone this boy to death
His mother sobbed as he was mobbed and took his final breath

Don't break the 4th commandment - that behavior's not condoned
And do not use God's name in vain - or you just might get stoned!

BIBLE VERSES: Leviticus 24:10-23

76

NUMBERS BIBLE POEMS

NUMBERS

So how did Numbers get its name? Because *that's what it is*
The answer to that question would be easy on a quiz
It's all about the Israelites - their tribes and their dependents
Some guy begat another guy - recording their descendants

Each family had its duties and they all would work together
Some worked inside the holy place - some worked out in the weather
The Gershonites had special tasks - the curtains and the ropes
All tabernacle hangings with their angles and their slopes

The Kohathites were all assigned to furniture inside
The lampstand and the altars and the ark they cleaned with pride
The Merarites just carried stuff - the posts, and bars and beams
And some of it was heavy so they probably worked in teams

The Hebronites, and Mushites and the Levites, and their clans
I could go on forever 'bout their duties and demands
Today we don't have all those "ites" - they soon would disappear
But termites and mosquito bites are always somewhere near

BIBLE VERSES
Numbers 1 - 4

THE PLIGHT OF A NAZARITE

The laws we see in Numbers often seem to be quite weird
A Nazarite, for instance, could not ever shave his beard
A razor could not touch his hair or even touch his head
And he could never go around a body that was dead

He couldn't visit funeral homes or cemetery lots
He couldn't guzzle alcohol or margarita shots
No vinegar could touch his lips and nothing from the vine
No raisins in his salad bowl when he went out to dine

He couldn't even have a grape or else his vow was sunk
At least his mom was not afraid that he would come home drunk
If someone dies while he's around it puts him in a jam
The Nazarite must shave his head and offer up a lamb

Then turtledoves or pigeons and a bunch of other stuff
It's hard to be a Nazarite, the rules are really tough
But after he has done all this, to help him realign
The priest will then encourage him to have a glass of wine!

I'm sure there was a Nazarite just hoping that someday
An older person standing near might choose to pass away
So if you're fond of raisins or you like to drink Coors lite
You just may not be qualified to be a Nazarite

BIBLE VERSES: Numbers 6

79

NOSE VOMIT

The Israelites complained about the food they had to eat
'Cause manna was their daily meal and they were craving meat
So, Moses was disgusted, and he let Jehovah know
"These dummies you have given me have caused a lot of woe"

"I'm sick of all these people - they all act like I'm their father
Why did you save these idiots? Why did you even bother?"
"They grumbled from the day we left - they built a golden cow
I'm sick and tired of leading them, so please – just kill me now"

I'm not exaggerating, that is really what he said
His cup was full from all their bull - he'd just as soon be dead
Then God spoke back to Moses, and he said, "I've heard their plea
If they are tired of manna, then I'll give a guarantee

For one full month I'll feed them quail 'til it runs out their nose
The meat will stick between their teeth, and some will decompose
And sure enough he sent the quail - it was a clever trick
For weeks that's all they had to eat and most of them got sick

And just as God predicted quail was dripping through their snout
Their sinus drainage was a mess, they couldn't blow it out
And some got stuck between their teeth where it would putrefy
And if you smelled their stinky breath you'd probably want to die

God sent his fire, and many died - a lesson would be learned
Be careful what you ask for if the answer gets you burned

BIBLE VERSES
Numbers 11

80

MIRIAM'S FOLLY

Now Miriam and Aaron didn't like the wife of Moses
She was from Ethiopia - they judged her – one supposes
For even way back there in time such prejudice existed
It seems that we just never learn how values can be twisted

Jehovah called them to his tent and then he made it plain
"You've criticized my chosen man and you have caused him pain"
So, Miriam would be consumed with leprosy that day
Her skin turned whiter than the snow and she was sent away

Then Aaron started shaking and his countenance was vexed
His sister was a leper and he feared that he was next
For seven days poor Miriam would be out there alone
Then God reached out to heal her and her leprosy was gone

It doesn't seem quite fair to me that Aaron sinned a lot
While others got their punishment, it seems that he did not
But one thing both of them would learn from scheming with each other
Was not to judge or criticize this man who was their brother

God warns us not to lay a hand on those he has anointed
And if we dare, we must prepare for judgment he's appointed

BIBLE VERSES
Numbers 12

WISE SPIES AND GUTLESS GUYS

As Moses and the Israelites got through the desert sand
The Lord said, "Moses, send some spies to check out Canaan land
Their leader would be Joshua - he was the son of Nun
Some said he had no father (Their attempt to make a pun)

And there was also Caleb - he's the second in command
To lead the spies, with their disguise into the promised land
For forty days and forty nights they wandered all around
And what they saw amazed them - it was really quite profound

They came back and reported that the cities had big walls
They brought back figs and even grapes the size of basketballs
"The promised land as God has said does flow with milk and honey
There's brooks and rivers everywhere, the weather is quite sunny"

"However, there are giants there that we cannot defeat"
And almost all the spies agreed, "In battle, we'd be beat"
But Joshua and Caleb both believed what God had said
And yes, indeed, they both agreed, "It's time to move ahead"

But guess what all the people did? They murmured once again
"We should return to Egypt; we were better off back then"
And once again Jehovah was about to wipe them out
And once again, ole Moses prayed (He really had some clout)

And once again, God would forgive, but this time he would say
"You could have entered Canaan but I'm sending you away"
"For forty years you'll wander 'round, and then you all will die
You'll never see the promised land - you do not qualify"

"But Joshua and Caleb and the young ones who believe
Will someday cross the Jordan and my promise, they'll receive"
"The rest of you, your carcasses will bleach out in the sun
The desert will consume you all before your life is done"

82

"And as for all the doubting spies, a plague will do you in
You doubted me, and you will be demolished for your sin
The people then decided that they'd enter Canaan land
But God withdrew his spirit, and they didn't understand

They thought that he'd be with them like he always was before
When Moses tried to warn them, his advice they would ignore
And all of them were foolish as they charged in for the kill
But Amalekites and Canaanites destroyed them on a hill

BIBLE VERSES: Numbers 14

KORAH'S CHALLENGE

God chose Aaron to become the high priest of the nation
He also chose the Levites for a special operation
The priests came from the Levite tribe; they had a special call
To handle all the holy things and minister to all

Now Korah was a Levite who got overly ambitious
He made some plans with two more guys that really were malicious
Dathan, Abiram, and Korah raised a rebel squad
Two hundred fifty leaders who set out to challenge God

They also challenged Moses and they said, "We're holy too
What makes you think you're special? 'Cause we're just as good as you"
Then Moses fell down on his face and asked God for direction
And God replied, "Here's what you do to stop this insurrection"

Take censors full of incense and go gather by my tent
And I will show the people that it's *you* that I have sent
Then Moses told the people who were milling all around
"The rebel leaders standing here will fall right through the ground"

The earth then separated and the rebels who had jeered
Both Korah and his buddies in an instant disappeared
And panic hit the people as they turned around to run
But God said unto Moses, "Hold your horses, I'm not done"

Two hundred fifty men succumbed as fire fell from the sky
They all had challenged Aaron's role and now these men would fry
You'd think by now the Israelites would listen and obey
Instead they kept complaining at the things God had to say

They all blamed Moses for the death of Korah and his crew
And God saw their rebellion and his anger quickly grew
He sent a plague throughout the land to everyone's dismay
And fourteen thousand, seven hundred died that very day

BIBLE VERSES: Numbers 16

NUTTY STAFF

Now Israel had 12 tribes of people, each tribe had a head
And sometimes jealousy arose as competition spread
Each leader owned a unique staff, their name was on the top
And Moses knew this rivalry and bickering must stop

And so, he asked them each to bring their staffs into the tent
And God would show whom he had chose - the man whom he had sent
The next day all the staffs were there, just leaning on the ark
But Aaron's staff had budded like a tree with leaves and bark

Not only had it budded, but some almonds grew there too
And Moses told the other guys, "I hope you get the clue"
'Cause their own staffs just sat there - nothing special had occurred
And Aaron's role was sealed that day by almonds and God's Word

Then Moses held the staff out and the arguments were stilled
But then it scared the people who cried out, "We'll all be killed"
Can you imagine working with these people all the time?
Their grumbling and complaining - their rebellion and their crime

The miracles that God performed, they witnessed every day
Yet time and time again they just kept doing things their way
But somehow God put up with them, his grace he would supply
I'm thankful that he does the same for folks like you and I

BIBLE VERSES: Numbers 17

85

MISSION UNACCOMPLISHED

The people all got thirsty, and they started up their moaning
Poor Moses once again would have to put up with their groaning
"Why did we leave the land of Egypt just to follow you?
This wilderness is hot and dry with snakes and scorpions too"

"And now we have no water, and our throats are raw and parched
If we knew then what we know now we never would have marched"
They all were standing near a rock that God had pointed out
He said, "I'll turn that boulder into one big waterspout"

"Just speak the word and water will gush out above your head"
But Moses still was angry, so he struck the rock instead
The water flowed but Moses failed - Jehovah was offended
And Moses knew that he was due to soon be reprimanded

His mission was disqualified for failing God's command
And now he could not lead them all into the promised land
And Miriam would die there - she'd be buried near that stone
Poor Moses lost his sister, and his mission now was gone

The place would be named "Meribah" for quarreling that took place
It would remain a memory of much failure and disgrace
One small misdeed can change the course that you pursue today
Be sure to keep your heart in tune and don't be led astray

BIBLE VERSES
Numbers 20:1-13

FAMILY FEUD

Some Israelites went over to engage the Edom clan
They asked the king's permission just to travel through his land
The Edomites were Esau's kids, all kin to one another
'Cause Israel came from Jacob who was Esau's younger brother

But Edom's king refused them with a strong and forceful "Nay"
He sent his army after them so they would go away
Instead of going through their land, they took another route
It saved a lot of trouble and a lot of lives, no doubt

But now a family feud would start with Israel and with Edom
Sometimes our cousins are a pain - that's when you just don't need 'em

BIBLE VERSES: Numbers 20:14-21

DECEASED HIGH PRIEST

Now Moses and his brother Aaron traveled to Mt. Hor
They knew that God had sent them there - they just weren't sure what for
Eleazor, Aaron's oldest son would come along
And Moses had an inkling that there might be something wrong

Then God revealed to Aaron that his earthly life was done
And so he took his priestly robes and put them on his son
The first high priest of Israel would forever be at peace
His priestly job was over, and his journey now would cease

BIBLE VERSES: Numbers 20:22-29

ISRAELITE SNAKE BITE

Once again, the Israelites would murmur and complain
These folks just never seemed to learn - they really were a pain
They gripped about the water, and they griped about the manna
And once again God picked them up on Heaven's big antenna

But this time when they ticked him off, he sent a bunch of snakes
They started biting everyone, and people got the shakes
Again, they turned to Moses, pleading mercy for their sin
This drama just kept happening - again –again –again

Jehovah gave instructions, "Make a serpent out of brass
And raise it high upon a pole, and it shall come to pass"
"That everyone who's bitten - when they gaze upon this snake
Will find that they are healed, and they can learn from their mistake"

But many died from snakebites, it is written in the book
Some idiots just passed away because they wouldn't look

BIBLE VERSES: Numbers 21:4-9

JUST LISTEN TO YOUR ASS

Now Balak, king of Moab was afraid of Israelites
He saw the damage they had done to all the Amorites
He'd heard about a prophet whose predictions brought him fame
He asked about - and figured out that Balaam was his name

And so, he tried to hire him as a mystic private eye
But Balaam heard from God, who said, "Don't listen to this guy"
So, Balaam sent a message back to Balak, saying "No"
But Balak still persisted, and he told his servants, "Go"

"Go bribe this stubborn prophet - be aggressive and be bold
And lavish him with costly gifts of silver, gems, and gold"
At first Balaam resisted, but he finally did give in
It's sad to know that wealth can cause a godly man to sin

So, Balaam got his donkey and they started back to town
When suddenly an angel would appear to slow them down
Now Balaam didn't see him - he was blinded by the money
But Balaam's ass, who had more class, just started acting funny

The donkey saw the angel and it tried to veer away
And Balaam tried to beat his ass, but it would not obey
His ass then turned and spoke to him, its voice was harsh, but low
"Just beat me all you want to, but I'm not about to go"

The angel stood there with a sword - the donkey stood its ground
With walls on either side of it, there was no way around
But Balaam now was angry, and he beat the donkey more
He screamed, "Quite acting like an ass, or I will make you sore!"

And then the donkey hunkered down, ignoring Balaam's threat
And with a smirk, it said, "You jerk, I'm not your household pet"
"I've always done what you have asked, but this time I won't dare
Are you so blind that you can't see that angel standing there?"

90

Then suddenly it dawned on him - "My ass is talking back
Not only is it talking, I believe its talking smack"
Then Balaam's eyes were opened, and he fell down on his face
And God said, "I should take your life, you're such a big disgrace"

"That donkey has more sense than you, three times it saved your bacon
If not for it you would be dead and totally forsaken"
"Now get back on your ass and I will tell you what to do
And if you mess up one more time, then I am through with you"

So, Balaam went to Moab, and he met with Balak there
And Balaam told the king, "What God commands – I will declare"
Now seven times King Balak would command he give a curse
And seven times Balaam replied, his answer would be terse

"I cannot curse what God has blessed; I'll only speak what's true"
King Balak walked away from him and said, "Okay, we're through!"
Now here's advice for Balaam whom Jehovah gave a pass
Next time your donkey talks to you - just listen to your ass

BIBLE VERSES: Numbers 22-24

91

BELLYACHE MISTAKE

While Israel stayed in Shittim all the men would misbehave
They flirted with the Moabites - their women they would crave
They all bowed down to idols, and they sacrificed to Baal
God's anger starting rising, and went off the Richter scale

And then a man named Zimri brought back home a Midianite
Phinehas, who had seen it all, got angry and uptight
He took a spear and followed them, and called Zimri a "dummy"
He then would jab him through the chest into the woman's tummy

Now Kozbi was the lady's name - that spear caused her to shake
Her tombstone said that she expired from one bad bellyache
And God was angry with them all - their sinfulness and pride
And so he sent a plague and over twenty thousand died

God honored young Phinehas who was of the Levite clan
And all of his descendants would be blessed through this one man
His dad was Eleazar, who was high priest at the time
These names are sometimes hard to say - especially in a rhyme!

BIBLE VERSES: Numbers 25

92

NUN FUN

Now Joshua was Catholic (And this joke is called a "pun")
He lived inside a convent, 'cause his father was a "Nun"

BIBLE VERSES: Numbers 27:18

TRANSITION

Now God called Joshua and Moses to a mountain peak
Now, Moses was an old man, but he really wasn't weak
And there, God would remind him that he could not enter in
The land that he had promised them because of Moses' sin

The time that he had smote the rock instead of speaking to it
There's more, but I just don't have time to take a person through it
Now Moses knew his time had come - he soon would pass away
A leader should be chosen sometime soon, if not today

God pointed out to Moses that young Joshua's the man
That he had chose to lead his people to the Promised Land
Now Moses knew his time had come - he'd lived life to the brim
He died upon the mountain top - and God would bury him

But God was not quite finished with this holy, faithful man
'Cause one day he and Jesus and Elijah all would stand
Upon another mountain top and witnesses were there
To tell the story of the glory all of us can share

BIBLE VERSES: **Nu. 27:12-22 Deut. 34:1-5 Matt. 17:1-4**

DEUTERONOMY BIBLE POEM

DEUTERONOMY

Deuteronomy is quite a word - the second giving of the law
That's what it means if you've not heard; pronouncing it may strain your jaw
It's full of lengthy regulations - feasts, and laws, and proclamations

Some say it's boring and absurd - especially since it does repeat
The things in Exodus we heard that really are a bit downbeat
But there is always bits of light in passages we may think trite

There are some stories you may like and some you have already read
So, you may rather take a hike and start with Joshua instead
But if you chose to read it through, there may be helpful things to view

BIBLE VERSES: Deuteronomy 1 - 34

JOSHUA BIBLE POEMS

97

THE HARLOT AND THE SCARLET CORD

The people cried when Moses died, and Joshua now led
He challenged all of Israel to begin to move ahead
The Promised Land before them and the wilderness behind
For forty years their parents had been faithless, crude, and blind

But this young generation had a vision to succeed
And they were ready to possess the Promised Land, indeed
And Joshua decided there were things that he must know
About the giant walls around the town of Jericho

Two trusted spies were sent at night to check out everything
A harlot hid them in her house, but someone told the king
And he sent soldiers to her home to capture those two guys
But Rahab, (she's the prostitute), would tell the soldiers lies

She told them that the spies were gone, and so they would withdraw
But Rahab hid them on her roof beneath a bed of straw
That night she told the two brave spies that people in her nation
Were all afraid of Israel and they lived in consternation

They'd heard about the parting of the waters in the sea
How Pharaoh's army all had drowned and Israel's victory
They knew through signs and miracles that God had Israel's back
And they now feared that they were next for Israel to attack

So, Rahab begged for mercy as she gave the spies a hand
She asked that all her family would be spared when it began
The spies then gave their promise, and they swore before their Lord
But Rahab must provide a sign and hang a scarlet cord

Outside the window of her home, and then, they both declared
That when the fighting started all her family would be spared
That scarlet cord would be the sign for Israelites to see
And when they captured others - Rahab's family would go free

98

She then would lower both the spies with ropes down to the ground
The next three days they hid up in the hills, lest they be found
They crossed the Jordan river with some good things they could tell
The folks in Jericho were scared and Israel would prevail

BIBLE VERSES
Joshua 1 - 2

CROSSOVER

The Red Sea was amazing stuff - a miracle divine
But when you read what happens next, it's sure to blow your mind
The time had come to enter Canaan - Israel was prepared
They'd take this land if they believed the things that God declared

However, there's a problem that they soon would realize
The Jordan River overflowed - it now was twice its' size
And they would have to cross it to get to the Promised Land
But Joshua was full of faith and firmly took command

He ordered twelve strong Israelites to go and get the ark
And put it on their shoulders as they started to embark
The ark would lead the entire camp down to the Jordan River
Where they would trust that once again, Jehovah would deliver

And when the priests were near the edge and moisture touched their toes
Dry land appeared before them as a wall of water rose
The Jordan River piled up high and backed up to a city
The name of it was "Adam" and I find that rather witty

The priests stood in the middle and the riverbed stayed dry
They held the ark for hours as the Israelites passed by
When everyone passed over, then the priests were last to go
And then the waters were released the river now could flow

The day that Jesus died for us, our sins were washed away
The backflow went to Adam, then ahead for us today
He is the ark – he is the priest - he makes the waters part
He is the way, the truth, the life - he's living in our heart

BIBLE VERSES:
Joshua 3   Hebrews 4:14   John 14:6

100

ROCKS IN THE RIVER

When Israel crossed the Jordan River - Joshua demanded
That one strong guy from every tribe would do as he commanded
He sent them to the river where they picked up twelve big boulders
Down where the men were standing with the ark up on their shoulders

So out into the riverbed these men would gather stones
The riverbed was drier than a stack of dusty bones
They carried them up to the bank and when the ark came out
The water started flowing and the people gave a shout

They hauled those stones to Gilgal where a monument they'd raise
And many generations would remember and give praise
The people had respect for Josh - they knew he would succeed
With Moses gone, Josh was the one who now could take the lead

The wilderness behind them, and the Jordan river too
The Promised Land before them, there was still a lot to do
The Israelites would face more fights - the going would be rough
They had no clue that one day you would read about this stuff

BIBLE VERSES: Joshua 4

101

OUCH!

At Gilgal God told Joshua to circumcise the guys
He helped them mentally prepare; for they would agonize
It goes back to the covenant God made with Abraham
(I'm sure the men would much prefer to offer up a lamb)

And so, the deed was finally done and, on their beds, and couches
They moaned and groaned and squirmed around through pain and lots of
"Ouches"
The place was then named Gilgal, for it caused a lot of pain
The memories there, I do declare, near drove them all insane

The healing process took a while - their moods were not too sunny
And when they got up out of bed, they walked a tad bit funny
Circumcision, like the rainbow, was a sign and symbol
One made you feel much safer, while the other made you tremble

BIBLE VERSES
Joshua 5:2-9

A PICTURE HERE
WOULD BE IN
APPROPRIATE!

102

NO MO' JERICHO

When Joshua neared Jericho, an angel would appear
A sword was in his hand, but he told Josh to have no fear
"Are you for us or against us?", was the question Josh would ask
The angel said, "I'm neither - but God sent me with a task"

He then told Josh, "Take off your sandals, this is holy ground
The walls of Jericho are strong, but they will be brought down"
"Just do what God requires of you and Jericho will fall
You then must cleanse the city with the sword by killing all"

Then Joshua commanded that for six days they would walk
Around the walls of Jericho, but none of them could talk
While seven priests blew trumpets, they were marching to the beat
I'm sure they all got callouses and blisters on their feet

Now this went on for six long days and nothing was occurring
The sun was hot, the ground was dry, I'm sure their eyes were blurring
But on the seventh day they all would go the extra mile
And circle seven times around - it probably took a while

And on the seventh time around the people gave a shout
The walls of Jericho fell down and crumbled all about
And all the people were destroyed, except for Rahab's kin
God honored her for helping hide the spies when they came in

Then Rahab and her family were provided for that day
The Israelites assigned a place for all of them to stay
And God commanded Joshua that nothing could be taken
The city would be burned, and then, forever be forsaken

The gold and silver they would find could not be used or spent
No warrior could possess it - to God's treasury it went
God put a curse on Jericho - he said that anyone
Who tried to build it up again would lose their firstborn son

BIBLE VERSES
Joshua 6

ACHAN'S FOLLY

Now Israel was unfaithful to - the things God asked for them to do
At Jericho he told them to abstain
From taking any gold or silver - they were not to steal or pilfer
Anything for their own personal gain

105

But Achan was a greedy man - and he would take some contraband
And hide it in the ground beneath his quilt
He blatantly had disobeyed - his greed had caused him to be swayed
And now he would be burdened down with guilt

When Joshua sent men to fight - the enemy put them to flight
And Josh knew something wasn't right, you see
'Cause Ai was a little town - that should be easy to put down
Instead, they caused the Israelites to flee

So, Joshua fell on his face - and begged the Lord to give them grace
But God said, "Josh, there's something you must do"
There's trouble in the camp today - and you must go and find a way
To punish Achan and his entire crew"

So Achan was confronted and - confessed that he and all his clan
Had stolen things from Jericho that day
Then several guys that Josh had sent - went barging into Achan's tent
And found the stuff that he had hid away

So Achan's family all were led - out to a valley where they bled
As other people stoned them all to death
A penalty was paid that day - they learned that stealing doesn't pay
As sadly each would draw their final breath

The valley where they died would be - renamed for all eternity
To "Achor" which means "Valley full of trouble"
Where Achan, who had thoughts of greed - would die for his ungodly deed
Now buried down beneath a pile of rubble

BIBLE VERSES: Joshua 7

AMBUSHED

Now after Achon had been stoned, Ai would be attacked
And this time Achon's sin would not cause Israel to be sacked
The first ambush in history would occur in this event
Jehovah gave them all a plan and then they all were sent

A group of soldiers snuck behind the city late at night
And early in the morning they would all join in the fight
Then Josh and all the other men approached the enemy
They lured them out the city walls and then began to flee

The warriors all from Ai thought they had them on the run
'Til soldiers slipped behind them, and the ambush had begun
They sandwiched in the enemy and all from Ai died
The victory was completed when the ambush was applied

They brought the king of Ai back to Joshua that day
And he impaled him on a pole and carried him away
At sunset they would throw him down beside the city gate
His kingship now was over 'cause an ambush sealed his fate

BIBLE VERSES: Joshua 8:1-28

107

THE PLIGHT OF THE "ITES"

The Israelites had enemies - they all were Canaanites
The Perizzites, the Jebusites, and then the Amorites
The Hittites and the Gibeonites were fearful for they knew
That God was with the Israelites - they'd seen what he could do

And so, the Gibeonites would trick the Israelites one day
They made them think that they had come from very far away
Their clothes were smelling musty, and their bread was dry with mold
Their coats were torn and dusty and their sandals were quite old

And Joshua was tricked into a treaty with these guys
They'd put on a performance that he soon would realize
They all agreed to live in peace since they were from afar
To honor this agreement and to never go to war

But after they had signed the thing, they came to understand
That they had been outwitted by this clever local clan
They now could never go to war, or harm the Gibeonites
It caused much agitation to these angry Israelites

But Gibeon had played a trick, and it was understood
That they would pay for their deceit by cutting all the wood
And carrying the water that the Israelites would need
It was a fair arrangement, and so everyone agreed

That they would cut down all the wood, and carry all the water
So, Joshua, who they had fooled, turned out to be much smarter

BIBLE VERSES
Joshua 9

PARALYZED SKIES

Five kings from Canaan were concerned about the Gibeonites
They heard how they were allies of those warring Israelites
And so, they all joined forces, and to Gibeon they went
They rallied all their troops and then, their armies all were sent

But Gibeon requested that the Israelites join in
To fight against these armies as an ally and a friend
So, Josh took his whole army and they marched throughout the night
Their unexpected presence made the enemy take flight

And as the kings and all their armies ran away from battle
Big hailstones pounded from the sky and made their helmets rattle
The hailstones were so huge - they killed more soldiers than the sword
The Israelites could sense a win and so their voices roared

And then something would happen that seemed eerie and unreal
'Cause Joshua would tell the sun and moon to both be still
The universe came to a halt - the sun just froze in place
For one full day there was no night - impacting time and space

And everyone who saw it took that memory to the grave
It scared the five rebellious kings who hid inside a cave
Then Josh told men to block the cave - the kings would be retained
Until the Israelites prevailed, and victory was obtained

The Gibeonites were thankful now that Israel was their friend
Because the kings and all their armies met a bitter end
Now meanwhile at the cave the rebel kings were brought outside
And Joshua would show his men how justice was applied

The kings were forced down on the ground - they were a nervous wreck
And Josh's leaders, with their feet, would stomp them on the neck
They killed the kings and hung them high, to dangle in the wind
To show their foes that if opposed, the Israelites would win

109

That day would be one of a kind as history would reveal
And not one warrior would forget the day the sun stood still

BIBLE VERSES
Joshua 10

THIRTY-ONE TO NOTHING

While Joshua led Israel, they would fight a lot of wars
Tens of thousands would be slain, while many more had scars
The total would be thirty-one, (the kings that would be killed)
Their kingdoms utterly destroyed - their peoples' voices stilled

The King of Hebron, King of Ai - King of Jericho
The King of Hepher, King of Lachish - King of Megiddo
King of Libnah, King of Bethel, Tirzah, Madon, Dor
Arad and Jerusalem, and many, many more

One by one they challenged Israel - but they paid the cost
One by one they entered battle - one by one they lost
Each battle would be different, but each battle had a story
Each battle had its ups and downs - each battle would be gory

In history there has only been one leader who has said
"I'm thirty-one and zero in the battles I have led"

BIBLE VERSES
Joshua 11-12

111

TWO LEGENDS

Caleb now was eighty-five - still quite a healthy man
He met with Joshua to see if he could own some land
The two of them for forty years had led the Israelites
They'd been through many battles as they fought the Canaanites

They both were in the group of spies that Moses first sent in
The only two that said they knew the Israelites could win
They both were getting older and were tired of all the wars
Their fighting days were over - it was time to heal their scars

So, Joshua blessed Caleb and he gave to him a town
So, Hebron would become his home where he would settle down
The final chapters in this book are all about the clans
And how God would assign to them allotment of the lands

Old Joshua would pass away - his goals had all been met
His fame would live forever as a man we'd not forget

BIBLE VERSES: Joshua 14 – 24

JUDGES BIBLE POEMS

THUMBS AND TOES

The men of Judah took the lead soon after Josh's end
They went to war with Canaanites and killed ten thousand men
They put the enemy to flight and left their town a wreck
The king was named Adoni and the town was called Bezek

They captured King Adoni, and they cut off his big toes
They also cut his thumbs off - it was gruesome, I suppose
He casually had mentioned that he'd done the same thing too
He'd chopped off royal thumbs and toes of kings that he once knew

It fact, he mentioned seventy - that's quite a lot of toes
And what he did with all their thumbs, I'm sure nobody knows
He chained them to his table, where they begged for scraps of food
These guys who lived in Bible times were sometimes really crude

They took him to Jerusalem, and there Adoni died
(I couldn't make these stories up - not even if I tried)
Jerusalem was defeated by the Israelites that day
The toeless, thumbless, former king, was finally put away

BIBLE VERSES: Judges 1

114

JUDGES

The generations came and went, and God was soon forgotten
Young people worshipped idols and their attitudes were rotten

An angel came to warn them that they soon would be oppressed
So, raiders came to plunder and the people were distressed

But God still loved his people, so he gave them gentle nudges
To keep them on a righteous path he ordained several judges

As long as judges guided them, they seemed to do okay
But things would fall apart when any judge would pass away

This cycle would continue, and it seemed they never learned
That when they chose to disobey, they always would get burned

BIBLE VERSES: Judges 2

THE FIRST THREE JUDGES

The first judge Israel ever had was Othniel, Caleb's brother
He won each battle Israel fought in one way or another
Because of him the fighting stopped, and order would increase
As long as Othniel was their judge, the nation lived in peace

But once he died, the Israelites reverted back to sin
And God let them get captured by the Moabites again
Now Eglon, King of Moab, kept them slaves for eighteen years
Until another judge arose to conquer all their fears

The second judge was Ehud - he would do as God commanded
Now Ehud would be famous as the first to be left-handed
He had a sword with double edges hidden on his thigh
He went to visit Eglon with a present for the guy

He left the king and headed home, but then he circled back
And asked to meet the king in private, just to sit and yak
King Eglon sent his servants out so he could meet with Lefty
He waddled back and settled down - the man was really hefty

Then Ehud drew his hidden sword and plunged it in his belly
King Eglon was so very fat - his stomach was like jelly
Then Ehud quickly left the king, whose life was now deleted
He rallied all the Israelites, and Moab was defeated

As second judge of Israel, he would make their bondage cease
And Ehud led for eighty years, and Israel lived in peace
When Ehud died a third judge came - a brave and noble man
He killed 600 Philistines that died by Shamgar's hand

The jawbone of an ass was used by Samson in his quest
But Shamgar used an oxgoad - it's the weapon he liked best
Three judges came, three judges went, and God was on their side
But Israel would continue on their roller coaster ride

BIBLE VERSES: Judges 3

JAY AND DEBBIE

Now once again Israel had sinned, and once again were slaves
They acted like a little child that always misbehaves
For twenty years they served the king of Canaan and his city
Oppressed and down they cried for help, and God would show them pity

He raised another judge for them, and Deborah was her name
But Debbie wasn't satisfied to let things stay the same
She soon would order Barak, who commanded Israel's men
To go and fight the Canaanites, and she assured a win

They soon encountered Sisera, the Canaanites great leader
He knew that Debbie was in charge and figured he could beat her
But Israel started winning, causing Sisera to run
His army was defeated, and his leadership was done

A friend named Jael lived nearby and so that's where he went
His legs were feeling shaky as he slipped into her tent
He hid beneath a blanket so if someone happened by
And asked if Jay had seen him, she could fabricate a lie

She brought some milk for him to drink, but what he didn't know
Was that Jael despised him - it was soon about to show
She took a hammer and a peg and drove it through his head
And then she sent for Barak just to show that he was dead

Then Deb and Barak sang a song to celebrate their win
Their army had defeated all the Canaanites again
The heroes weren't just mighty men who always won the fight
This time Jael and Debbie were the ones who did it right

BIBLE VERSES: Judges 4-5

SMALL IS BETTER

Jehovah sent a prophet to rebuke the Israelites
They all were captured once again - this time by Midianites
He pointed out the repetition, leading to defeat
From bondage to deliverance - and the cycle would repeat

This time the judge was Gideon - a meek and lowly man
In fact, he said himself that he was weakest in his clan
An angel would appear to him and startled him, indeed
He said, "Oh mighty warrior, God has chosen you to lead"

"Excuse me," Gideon replied, "Did you say that to me?
I am the weakest of the weak, as anyone can see"
"If you are really who you say, then prove it on your own"
He went and got some bread and meat and placed them on a stone

The angel touched the meat and bread, and fire leaped from the rock
And then the angel disappeared - with Gideon in shock
He screamed out loud, "Alas, my Lord, I've seen you face to face"
And God said, "Do not be afraid, I've called you by my grace"

But Gideon began to doubt that God had really spoken
And so, he pleaded with the Lord to give a sign or token
He placed a fleece out on the ground and made a proposition
"Tomorrow if this fleece is wet then I'll accept my mission"

"But make the ground around it dry and then I'll really know
That I am called to lead the fight and I will gladly go"
And so, the Lord did what he asked - the fleece was wringing wet
But Gideon still doubted, and he wasn't quite done yet

He prayed, "Have mercy on me Lord - but give me one more try
Please have the ground be sopping wet, but let the fleece be dry"
God rolled his eyes and then replied, "Okay, but this is it
Just one more time I'll play the game - but then you must commit"

119

And so, the process was reversed, and Gideon believed
He knew that God was on his side, and he was quite relieved
So early the next morning tens of thousands made their way
They came to fight the Midianites, but God showed up to say

"Your army has too many men - I thought I'd let you know
Tell anyone that is afraid that they are free to go"
Now over twenty thousand left and headed back to town
Ten thousand men were left to fight, but God still wore a frown

He said, "If Israel wins the fight, they'll think that they are wise
I want for them to know it's me - and not their strength or size"
"So, take them to the water and observe their drinking style
The ones who cup their hands to drink are chosen from this trial"

"The ones who lap it like a dog will have to leave today"
Three hundred men would cup their hands - three hundred men would stay
God told them to take trumpets - and take torches in some jars
And go surround the Gideonites at night beneath the stars

And when the trumpets sounded, they would smash the jars they held
The light would glow, and they would know, the moment they all yelled
That God had given victory to the Israelites that night
The enemy was so confused, they ran around in fright

They turned against each other, and the slaughter would begin
While Gideon and his small crew just watched them with a grin
Two Midianite commanders left the camp, and they were joggin'
When soldiers from the Israelites would sever off their noggin

The lesson Israel learned was that no matter what we do
It's not by might nor power, but it's God who brings us through
God's strength will be made manifest through all our human weakness
His thoughts and ways are not our own - revealing His uniqueness

BIBLE VERSES: Judges 6-7

120

THE WIMP IS A WARRIOR

Three hundred men with Gideon, pursued the Midianites
As thousands ran from this small band of chosen Israelites
And when they came to Sukkoth, Gideon would ask for bread
To feed his band of hungry men, and help them move ahead

However, Sukkoth told him "No" - that's all they had to say
And Gideon would warn them all that soon they'd have to pay
He said, "Because you wouldn't help my soldiers here in need
We'll come back here and rip your flesh with thorns until you bleed

From there they went to Peniel where again they answered "No"
Now twice the men had been refused - so on the road they'd go
But Gideon replied that on the day and on the hour
When he returned, he'd kill the men - and then destroy their tower

A hundred twenty thousand men would die that fateful day
And just three hundred weary men would cause this massive fray
Then Gideon returned back to the towns that told him "No"
He ripped the men at Sukkoth with sharp thorns and blood did flow

He then went back to Peniel, and he tore their tower down
His warriors took their swords and then killed every man in town
He'd captured two strong Midianites - these dudes were really bad
He told his son to kill them, but the boy was just a lad

These two then started taunting him - they said, "Why don't *you* try?"
So, Gideon accepted, and he caused both dudes to die
This under-rated coward who had viewed himself as meek
Was transformed to a mighty warrior - all within a week

BIBLE VERSES: Judges 8

ABIMELEK THE WRECK

Abimelek was quite a dude - this son of Gideon was crude
He hired some sleazy guys to kill his brothers
All seventy were harshly thrown and murdered on a single stone
They shared their dad, but all had different mothers

Now Jotham was the youngest son, and when he saw what had been done
He ran away and climbed a mountain peak
He told the folks a tale of trees and warned them that they couldn't please
His brother, who was known to be a freak

He spoke about an olive tree, that all the trees had chose to be
Their king – But then the olive tree replied
"I'd rather give my oil away than acting like a king today
'Cause royalty is not my thing", it sighed

The fig tree then was asked and said, "I'd rather give my fruit instead
Of sitting on a high and mighty throne"
The trees then asked the sprawling vine - but it would rather give its wine
They finally asked the thorn bush, with a groan

The thorn bush smiled and then agreed that it would be their king indeed
As long as they all lingered in its shade
The thorn bush was a useless scrub and Jotham's tale was quite a rub
His brother was the thorn bush renegade

Then Jotham fled and lived in Beer, (Not Coors or Bud, just to be clear)
That was the city where he chose to hide
He knew his brother very well - he hated him, and he could tell
Abimelek would hunt him 'til he died

Abimelek would rule and reign for three short years, he was a pain
To everyone who got to know this guy
To make this story short and quick - he made the people 'round him sick
And most of them just hoped that he would die

123

One day his army showed their power - chasing folks into a tower
They all locked the door and tried to hide
Abimelek would then conspire - he told his guys to build a fire
And torch the place 'til all of them were fried

But one young lady climbed up high and out the window she let fly
A millstone that was like a chunk of lead
Abimelek was just below - that stone would give his head a blow
It cracked his skull, and he was nearly dead

He told his servant, "Take your sword and run me through – I can't afford
For folks to think a woman caused my death"
And so the servant did his best and stuck that sword right through his chest
And watched his master take his final breath

BIBLE VERSES: **Judges 9**

124

GRANPA DODO

Abimelech was dead and gone
And Tola would obtain the throne
His grandpa's name was Dodo – that's no joke
For twenty-three long years he reigned
From fighting wars, he had refrained
And then like all the judges, he would croak

And after Tola, Jair appeared
His thirty sons he loved and reared
They each one owned a donkey which they rode
They each controlled their own small town
In which they rode their donkeys 'round
That's all the info that the scriptures showed

Now after these two judges died
The Israelites once more denied
Jehovah – and were conquered once again
The Philistines and Ammonites
Would capture all the Israelites
For eighteen years they suffered for their sin

These Israelites just never learned
They first embraced and then they spurned
The God who had provided all their needs
I hope we learn from their mistakes
And can avoid their pains and aches
And honor Him in all our words and deeds

BIBLE VERSES: Judges 10

AWFUL OATH

Now Jephthah was a mighty man - his brothers, you must understand
Abandoned him and left him destitute
His father's name was Gilead - he cheated on his wife, it's sad
And Jephthah's mother was a prostitute

He left his home and quit his job, and moved into the land of Tob
A shady bunch would follow him around
One day a group of Israelites asked him to fight the Ammonites
And lead them as commander of their town

"You were the ones who kicked me out, so please bear with me if I doubt
The promise that you'll make me your commander"
They promised he'd be treated right if he would come and help them fight
They asked him to forgive them for their slander

So, he agreed to go to war - and things were looking up so far
'Til Jephthah made a deadly oath and swore
That if God helped them all to win, he'd sacrifice to Him again
The first one who ran out of his front door

And so, they fought the Ammonites - in twenty towns they won the fights
And Jephthah and his men were very glad
At home the people praised his fame - but out the door his daughter came
To celebrate the victory with her dad

She was the only child he had, and Jephthah now was very sad
He told her what he'd promised he would do
She told him he must keep his word, but asked if it could be deferred
For just two months so she could think it through

126

She took her friends and they would go into the hills where tears would flow
But her determination did not falter
She knew her dad now must obey - when she got home, they went away
Where he would take and burn her on an altar

BIBLE VERSES: Judges 11

DEADLY LISP

The Ephriamites were real upset
Their expectations were not met
When Jephthah went and fought the Ammonites
They told him they would burn his house
And kill him and his lovely spouse
'Cause he had not involved them in those fights

So, Jephthah took the Gileadites
And fought against those Ephriamites
And captured all the crossings to the Jordan
The Ephriamites were beaten bad
And they made Jephthah fuming mad
So, he refused to give them any pardon

The Ephriamites could not quite say
The letter "H" which fades away
Whenever they would speak a word like "show"
The "H" would disappear somehow
Their lisp would simply not allow
The "H" and it would always sound like "so"

So, Jephthah gave his guards a code
To capture Ephriamites who rode
On trails down near the Jordan River banks
The person must say "Shibboleth"
If they pronounced it "Sibboleth"
The guards would kill that person with their shanks

Now you may think it quite absurd
That folks could not pronounce that word
But you'd be wrong, I'm sorry to convey it
Such death and sorrow it would bring
That lisp would cost them everything
'Cause over forty thousand couldn't say it

128

So, if you are from Gilead
And have a lisp, I think it's bad
For you to ever venture by the river
'Cause if you say the code word wrong
Then I'm afraid it won't be long
Before a sword will slice right through your liver

Soon Jephthah met with his demise
And three more judges would arise
Ibzan, Elon, and Abdon came and went
Not much is said about these three
So, I'll be brief, as you can see
They didn't leave me stories to present

BIBLE VERSES: Judges 12

DISAPPEARING STRANGER

Manoah had a Danite wife who'd never had a child
A stranger would appear to her and tell her something wild
He said to her, "You'll have a son - he'll be a Nazarite
He must not drink champagne or wine - no Bud and no Coors lite"

"A razor cannot touch his head - his hair cannot be cut"
At first, she thought this unknown guy was really quite a nut
"What is your name?", they asked the man - he smiled and then replied
"You could not understand my name - not even if you tried"

Manoah and his wife would then go sacrifice a goat
The stranger jumped into the fire and upward he would float
He disappeared into the sky, and suddenly they knew
The stranger was an angel, and the things he said were true

They stood amazed by what they saw - both anxious and reflecting
But soon their doubts would fade away, 'cause soon she was expecting!
And so, this couple had a son - his strength would bring him fame
They raised him as a Nazarite, and Samson was his name

BIBLE VERSES: Judges 13

130

THE RIDDLE

Samson would fall for a Philistine girl
She was pretty but just a bit snappy
Now Israel was ruled by the Philistines then,
And his family was not very happy

They wanted their son to get married
But then – they wanted an Israelite bride
But Samson was stubborn and wouldn't relent
He threw all their wishes aside

He took them to Timnah to meet her one day
And while they were walking the path
An angry young lion, would charge from the field
And unleash on Samson his wrath

His parents had walked on ahead of their son
They never saw what had transpired
For Samson would tear that poor lion apart
And watch as he quickly expired

Now many days later while he was alone
He passed by the carcass again
Some bees had made honey and he ate his fill
'Till some of it dripped off his chin

Now Samson would marry the Philistine lass
And then he would throw a big feast
The Philistines sent thirty men to attend
The size of the party increased

Then Sam gave a riddle that only he knew
A riddle that no one would get
He gave them a challenge; he knew he would win
And buttered it up with a bet

He said, "From the eater there's something to eat
And out of the strong, something sweet"
Now no one else knew of the lion and bees
So, Samson knew he had them beat

For three days they pondered and worked on the riddle
They failed in their efforts – but then
They went to his wife, and they threatened her life
And forced her to help them to win

She pleaded with Samson to tell her the riddle
She whined and she pouted and cried
He finally gave in to her begging and pleading
His nerves and his patience were fried

She ran to the guys, and she gave them the answer
And when they saw Samson again
He knew he'd been had, and it made him so mad
That he went out and killed thirty men

He knew that his wife had deceived him, of course
And now he would stay with his dad
His wife would forsake him and marry again
The whole thing was really quite sad

BIBLE VERSES: Judges 14

132

FLAMING FOXES

When Samson learned that his new bride
Had married someone else, he cried
And in a rage, he went right off the rails
He caught three hundred foxes, then
He paired them off, and with a grin
He lit a torch and stuck it in their tails

The foxes ran through fields of grain
All trying to escape the pain
Of fiery flames they felt on their behinds
They burned down all the corn and wheat
While running on their blistered feet
And then destroyed the olive groves and vines

The Philistines felt consternation
When they saw the devastation
All would try to take poor Samson's life
But he escaped, which made things worse
'Cause someone else would feel the curse
They lit her house and burned his former wife

BIBLE VERSES
Judges 15:1-6

133

WEAPONIZED JAWBONE

After angry Philistines had burned and killed his bride
Ole Samson knew they wanted blood, so he commenced to hide
He found a cave inside a rock, and settled in a while
The Philistines were angry, and their attitudes were vile

They looked for him in Judah, and the threat was very clear
Three thousand men from Judah went to Samson out of fear
They said, "You must surrender or our families all will die"
So, Samson understood, and gave his hands for them to tie

They tied his hands with brand new ropes and led him from the cave
The Philistines intended now to put him in the grave
But then the Lord anointed him - he ripped those ropes apart
The Philistines were now afraid - the massacre would start

He saw a donkey's carcass and he reached down in the grass
Then slew a thousand warriors with the jawbone of an ass
And Samson now was thirsty from the battle he had fought
He asked God for some water - and a miracle was wrought

God opened up a hollow place, and water was provided
His thirst was quenched – his strength returned - his future was decided
For twenty years as judge he reigned - and led the nation well
Until Delilah came along - but that's another tale

BIBLE VERSES: Judges 15:8-20

134

SLEAZY DATES AND HEAVY GATES

Now Samson liked to hang around with ladies who would drag him down
The Philistines begin to understand
For Samson to disintergrate, their women were the perfect bait
And so, they got together, and they planned

He went to see a prostitute - the Philistines were quite astute
They gathered near the room when it got late
But in the middle of the night, he felt that something wasn't right
And headed out toward the city gate

And grabbing gates, he tore them loose, with muscles bulging like a moose
The posts and bars were also ripped away
He put them on his shoulders bare and climbed a hill and left them there
The Philistines were left in disarray

The enemy would lose that day - and let their foe just walk away
But there was still one lady yet to come
That story with its entire text - will be the one that you hear next
For Samson would be weakened, blind, and numb

BIBLE VERSES: Judges 16:1-3

135

FATAL ATTRACTION

Since Samson was a lady's man, the Philistines had made a plan
Delilah would become the perfect bait
They offered her a lot of dough if she would help them get to know
How they could break this man they'd come to hate

And so, she teased him playfully - she said, "Just place your trust in me
And tell me all the secrets to your power"
He teased her and he told her things, like "Tie me up with fresh bowstrings
Then I will lose my strength within the hour"

And so the bowstrings were provided - and the Philistines decided
They would help to implement this scheme
When Samson came, he took a nap, and while he lay there on her lap
She tied him up and then she gave a scream

He came awake and with a twist, he broke those bowstrings off his wrist
Delilah then began to pout and cry
She said, "You don't believe in me, and anyone can plainly see
That if you loved me, you would never lie"

Then Samson lied to her again, and told her with a wicked grin
"Just tie me up with brand new ropes and see
My strength would fade like shifting sand, and I would be a normal man
So please don't *ever* use new ropes on me"

Of course, that's what she went and did - and Samson, like a little kid
Just playfully annoyed her with a grin
He broke the ropes when she cried out, and laughed as she began to pout
Accusing him of failing her again

"For you to take my strength," he said, "Make seven braids atop my head
And pin them with the fabric in a loom"
So once again Delilah tried - her words were carefully applied
In hopes that she would help him face his doom

136

And once again he'd pulled a prank - and she would turn into a crank
And nagged 'til he was weary to the bone
He said, "If you should cut my hair - I speak the truth and do declare
That all my strength and power will be gone

And so, they shaved his head that night, and when he woke he couldn't fight
For he was weak and there was no reaction
They gouged his eyes and 'till he was blind
I'm sure he thought within his mind
"I made a fatal choice with this attraction"

BIBLE VERSES
Judges 16:4-21

(3 Samson Limericks)

THE FOX AND THE LOCKS

Now Samson was built like a tower - he made all his enemies cower
His gal was a fox - she cut off his locks
And Samson would lose all his power

WEAK AND BLEAK

Now Samson was big as a bear - his girlfriend would cut off his hair
His strength was now gone - and he was alone
'Cause they would break up their affair

BAD DATE

Delilah was Philistine bait - when Samson showed up for a date
She tricked him instead - and messed with his head
His hair would end up on a plate

BIBLE VERSES: Judges 16:4-21

GOODBYE SAMSON

Poor Samson lost his hair and eyes
A victim of Delilah's lies
In prison he worked hard at grinding grain
In shackles he would walk around
His muscles ached – the sweat poured down
Such torture that could drive a man insane

The Philistines, of course, were pagan
Worshipping a god called Dagon
He was half a fish and half a man
One day they went to sacrifice
And they did something not so nice
These Philistines had hatched an evil plan

They went and drug poor Samson out
To ridicule and laugh and shout
In front of Dagon, they would celebrate
But now his hair was getting longer
Samson knew that he was stronger
And the crowd discovered it too late

Between two columns made of stone
Ole Samson stood there all alone
He raised his voice to heaven, and he pleaded
"Dear God, please help me just once more
And make me stronger than before
And let these Philistines all be defeated"

And with a mighty push and groan
His strength began to crack the stone
The temple roof collapsed and took a dive
And thousands died that fateful day
With Samson, they all passed away
In death he killed more than he had alive

BIBLE VERSES: Judges 16:21-31

THE MAN WHO ROBBED HIS MOM

Now Micah lived up in the hills
He seemed to have such little skills
That he would steal some silver from his mother
But he would bring the silver back
(This guy was really quite a quack)
And they sat down and talked with one another

She blessed him with a nice reward
It seemed that she had no regard
That Micah was the one who took the money
There's something really fishy here
And I am sorry, but I fear
That Micah and his mom were acting funny

So, Micah took his mother's cash
(Which I still think was rather brash)
And made himself an idol and a shrine
He then ordained his son to be
A priest – which only proves to me
That there was something wrong with Micah's mind

A Levite came from Bethlehem
And found that he was in a jam
He had no money and no place to stay
Then Micah said "Let me pay you
To stay with me and if you do
You'll be an ordained priest this very day

And so, the Levite joined the team
But things got weirder it would seem
Five Danites came to visit them one day
They asked around and told some lies
No one suspected them as spies
And then they all would go their merry way

141

They went back where their tents were placed
And told their leader what they faced
He sent his troops out early the next day
They stole the idol and the shrine
They didn't leave a thing behind
They even took the Levite priest away

Then Micah rallied up some guys
But it would come as no surprise
That they were way outnumbered from the start
So, Micah and his crew would leave
The Danites just could not believe
That Micah and his friends were very smart

As you can see, I took the time
To make a lot of stories rhyme
And some of them were odd if you'll recall
But out of all the ones I've wrote
This story really got my goat
It was, by far, the strangest one of all!

BIBLE VERSES: Judges 17 - 18

142

OBTUSE ABUSE

A Levite and his concubine were headed home one day
They'd traveled far from Bethlehem and had no place to stay
An older man came from the fields and took them home to eat
They ate and started for the bed because they both were beat

But then a rowdy crowd appeared - a group of Benjamites
They took the concubine away and they abused her rights
And in the morning,, she was dead - her body was a mess
Her master took her home with him - it caused him much distress

He then did something frightening that no one had done before
He cut her up in pieces and he did a whole lot more
He sent the pieces to the tribes, and told them what was done
The Israelites were angry, and they unified as one

Four hundred thousand Israelites were armed and sent to fight
Disgusted by the Benjamites who'd caused this awful plight
Because one lady was abused, a massacre took place
And 90,000 warriors died, and fell upon their face

Revenge would be distributed by all the Israelites
They'd burn up all the cities of those rowdy Benjamites
One thoughtless deed, one violent act, can start an ugly war
But kindness and compassion have been known to travel far

BIBLE VERSES: Judges 19-20

STOLEN BRIDES

The Israelites had made an oath - their daughters must refrain
From marrying a Benjamite - for whom they had distain
Eleven tribes were unified - with Benjamin left out
The other tribes had punished them - there wasn't any doubt

But finally, peace would reign again, though something wasn't right
So many wives had lost their lives when Israel came to fight
The women of the Benjamites were far and few between
The other tribes had sworn an oath, and though it seemed quite mean

They couldn't let their daughters go and marry Benjamites
The covenant could not be broke, among the Israelites
They all made a suggestion that the Benjamites would try
Each year there was a festival with ladies standing by

These ladies were not Israelites and so they qualified
To be the wives of Benjamites who would not be denied
And so, the men hid in the trees to watch the ladies dance
They ran out there and grabbed one every time they had a chance

And then they took them back to town - I'm sure they fought and cussed
It took a while for them to smile and finally to adjust
It's not the greatest way to find the perfect bride for you
But when you're short on women what's a single guy to do?

BIBLE VERSES: Judges 21

RUTH BIBLE POEMS

ORPAH AND OPRAH

Naomi's husband passed one day - they lived in Moab, far away
She had two sons and both of them would die
And sorrow would enclose her heart – her life had fallen all apart
And all that she could do was sit and cry

The girls who married her two sons were widows now who had no funds
The first one's name was Orpah - then there's Ruth
Now Oprah Winfrey got her name from Orpah, yes, the very same
So, check it out and you'll find it's the truth

Naomi chose to up and scram, and head back home to Bethlehem
One day while with the girls she let it slip
And Orpah wished her all the best, but Ruth would make a firm request
That she could join Naomi on the trip

At first Naomi told her "No", but Ruth insisted that she go
She said, "Your God and people will be mine"
She then went on to plead her case, and so Naomi showed her grace
She finally did give in and told her "Fine"

Naomi felt depressed and low, and changed her name to "Mara" so
That everyone would know that she was bitter
When they arrived at her hometown - the harvest time had rolled around
And all the fields of grain were quite aglitter

In Moab Orpah lived and died - her history would be cast aside
'Til one day back in 1954
A teenaged girl would have a child and name her "Orpah" – ain't that wild!
But that's not all my friend, there's so much more

'Cause people got it all confused and called her "Oprah" so she used
That name, from then on out as we well know
I found this out through research time - since I'm the author of this rhyme
And also 'cause I've been on Oprah's show

If I'd go back in time today and meet with Orpah I would say
"Although for many centuries you've been gone
Someday, and through another's fame
The world will hear about your name
"You died and never dreamed that you'd live on"

So, we all know of Ruth today - and Orpah - through a long delay
God's timing isn't yours – you understand
The Lord will use you in His time - and as you've learned within this rhyme
He's never in a hurry with his plan

BIBLE VERSES
Ruth 1

147

BOAZ IS SMITTEN

Naomi had a "next-of-kin" - Boaz was known among the men
As quite a wealthy man with fields of wheat
Now Ruth decided she would go and help Naomi earn some dough
And so, she went to work out in the heat

She gleaned behind the workers where she gathered what was lying there
And then the owner of the fields arrived
He saw that Ruth was really cute and being single and astute
He came up with a plan that he contrived

He went to Ruth and with a smile, he said, "Just stay around awhile
And I'll make sure that you get what you need"
And when his workers came to dine, he gave her water, bread, and wine
Boaz was really smitten, yes, indeed

He told his men to treat her kind and leave some wheat and grain behind
And so, his workers honored his request
Now Boaz treated gleaners well, but Ruth as anyone could tell
Was treated much more kindly than the rest

When she got home with all that wheat, Naomi knew that something neat
Had happened – Something good but rather strange
And when she heard what Boaz did - her radar went right off the grid
She said to Ruth, "Your life's about to change"

Naomi told her with a smile, "You'll stay with me for just a while
But I can smell a wedding in the air"
She gave young Ruth some good advice - her words of wisdom were concise
The next poem tells us where it went from there

BIBLE VERSES
Ruth 2

FLIRTIN' FOR CERTAIN

Boaz had his eye on Ruth - Naomi knew that was the truth
So, she told Ruth, "You need to be asserting
So, go and get yourself decked out, 'cause he likes you, there is no doubt
It's time for you to do a little flirting"

Naomi told her what to do, and Ruth agreed to follow through
That night while Boaz finished counting sheep
She crept up to the place he lay - a threshing floor with scraps of hay
And at his feet she nestled in to sleep

It startled Boaz quite awake - he probably thought a rattlesnake
Had crawled beneath his blanket while he slept
But when he saw that Ruth was there, he whispered, "Well, I do declare
The moment I first saw you my heart leapt"

She lay there 'til the crack of dawn - he whispered, "You had best be gone
Before the other workers come awake"
He took the shawl that she now wore and into it much grain he'd pour
He gave her all the food that she could take

But in the night, he told her this, "There's someone who I cannot dis
A kinsman who by law could claim you first
If he declines, I'm happy then, 'cause I would gladly take you in
So let me see if he can be coerced"

So Ruth went home with all that food - Naomi saw her attitude
And knew that things were going just as planned
She said, "Be patient, wait and see - for Boaz wants this thing to be
He will redeem the right to take your hand

Now friend if you are in suspense - just know that this will all make sense
Like going to a movie on romance
Two fall in love, a problem comes - the hero beats up all the bums
They marry and the credits all advance

BIBLE VERSES
Ruth 3

SCHEMER AND REDEEMER

Now Ruth and Boaz were in love, there's wasn't any doubt
But just like in the movies, problems always seem to sprout
An elder kinsman had first rights to buy Naomi's land
But he was married, and his wife would never understand

Because whoever bought the land would get Ruth in the deal
And when his wife found out - she would be mad enough to kill
So, Boaz, who was next in line had turned into a schemer
He understood to marry Ruth, he must be her redeemer

And so, the first man then declined, and off his sandal came
Back then when business had transpired that's how they sealed the game
Boaz and Ruth were married - their descendants would be blessed
And Jesus would be one of them - so now you know the rest

But first they had a great-grandson who'd sit upon a throne
The greatest king of Israel - as King David would be known
The second kinsman paid the price and purchased Ruth with pride
From Adam, Christ redeemed us and received us as his bride

BIBLE VERSES: Ruth 4

151

OTHER BOOKS BY DARRELL SCOTT
Go to Amazon

Darrell Scott has authored, or co-authored 15 published books, including the best-seller, _Rachel's Tears_, the story of his daughter Rachel, the first victim of the Columbine high school shootings.

Darrell and his wife Sandy started a non-profit organization called, _Rachel's Challenge_, in Rachel's memory. Through its 50 presenters, Rachel's Challenge has reached over 28 million people in live settings over the last 18 years.

Rachel's Challenge has won 3 Emmy Awards through its television partners. They partner with Chuck and Gena Norris by providing character programming for the Norris's "KickStart Kids" organization. They also partner with the Cal Ripken, Sr. Foundation as well as with Marzano Research, one of the most prestigious K-12 research firms in the nation.

Darrell has appeared on numerous television programs such as Oprah, Larry King Live, Good Morning America, Dateline, O'Reilly Factor, Anderson Cooper, etc. He has been featured on the cover of Time magazine and quoted in Newsweek, the Wall Street Journal, and many other publications.

Darrell does keynote addresses for leadership teams of such organizations as Southwest Airlines, Bank of America, Sprint, BNSF Railroad, Motorola, and many others. He has met with Presidents Clinton, Bush, and Trump several times.

Darrell and his wife, Sandy, live in Lone Tree, Colorado where they enjoy their children and grandchildren.

Go to Amazon

 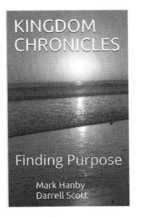 

  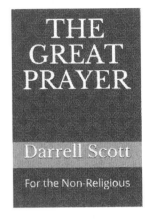

Go to: Amazon

Made in the USA
Columbia, SC
18 September 2023

23003468R00085